Extensions

Extensions

Adam Mornement

Laurence King Publishing

Published in 2007

by Laurence King Publishing Ltd

361–373 City Road

London

EC1V 1LR

E-mail: enquiries@laurenceking.co.uk

www.laurenceking.co.uk

Text © Adam Mornement 2007

This book was produced by Laurence King Publishing Ltd

A catalogue record for this book is available from
the British Library.

ISBN-10: 1-85669-494-1

ISBN-13: 978-1-85669-494-0

Designed by John Round Design

Edited by Mark Fletcher

Printed in China

Contents

1

1 Hoffman House, London, UK (1989–1992).
The world's first all-glass rear extension was built in
Hampstead, North London. The design, developed
collaboratively by architect Rick Mather, engineer
Tim MacFarlane and builder Pat Carter, has spawned
countless imitators. The landmark frameless double-
glazed lean-to was designed to meet the challenge
of improving connections between the kitchen and
the garden. A further innovation was the use of glass
panels with an invisible heat-reflecting film.

Introduction

**Memoirs of an imaginary home,
1907–2007**
Number 17 Lawn Lane, a mid-terrace 'two
up, two down', was built in four months
during the summer of 1907, towards
the end of the construction boom that
transformed Brookfield from a sleepy
suburb into a poor inner-city district.

The Wainrights were the first residents.
On the first Friday of every month, Ronald,
a 29-year-old father of three, paid rent to
the local docks, his landlord and employer.
The children all shared a bedroom; Grandma
slept downstairs. Wednesday-night baths
were taken in the kitchen. The toilet was a
shed at the end of the small rear courtyard.

It was the demise of cotton imports
that precipitated Brookfield's decline. When
the docks closed, it was a neighbourhood
stripped of purpose. By the beginning of the
1930s it was a slum.

Mr and Mrs Goldberg, a couple in their
fifties, bought Number 17 for a pittance in
1933. Over the next 23 years they added a
lean-to toilet onto the kitchen, converted
the courtyard into a vegetable patch
and turned the second bedroom into a
rudimentary bathroom. Lawn Lane had
never known such luxury.

The mid-1950s arrival of refugees from
war-torn East Africa gave Brookfield a new
lease of life. For the first time in decades,
children were seen playing on the street;
neighbours spoke to each other.

The Diars moved into Number 17 in
1957. The extended family included Dr Diar,
his wife, their four children, two cousins
and all four grandparents. The house was
bursting at the seams.

Every available space was colonized.
The void created by the pitched roof was
converted from a dark storage space into
the children's bedroom. There was no
insulation, and Dr Diar's self-designed
skylight seemed to act as a magnet for
the bitter winter winds. But the children's
complaints fell on deaf ears.

In 1964, Dr Diar bought Number 15
Lawn Lane and knocked the two houses
into one. A local builder removed the
party walls and converted the doorway of
Number 15 into a window. The work was
done quickly and on a limited budget, but it
was structurally sound, and the answer to
the Diars' prayers. The expanded Number 17
remained in the Diar family until 1988, when
Josh passed away, still complaining about
those cold winter nights in the loft space.

The current owners are Tristan and
Charlotte deHarthog, architects in their early
forties, who bought the house in 1992. Back
then Brookfield was still a byword for urban
squalor. The long-mooted underground
rail link that would 'regenerate' the area
remained a pipe dream. But the deHarthogs
were entranced. Number 17, by then a
partially derelict warren of dark, small
rooms with no central heating and with

suspicions of subsidence in the rear façade,
was all that they'd ever dreamed of. It was a
blank canvas: an opportunity to experiment.

The house was stripped to its bare
bones. All references to previous residents
were removed. A structural engineer friend
came round to advise on the subsidence.
The solution was to underpin the house and
build new foundations. In the process the
deHarthogs decided to dig out a basement,
adding a whole new floor which became a
kitchen and dining area with views over the
newly sunken garden through full-height
sliding doors.

Over the years an insulated lean-
to has been added to the rear, a deck
built in the landscaped garden, and solar
panels installed on the roof, providing
insulation and reducing energy costs. Inside,
floorboards have been laid and the original
brickwork sandblasted and left exposed.

It wasn't just the house that changed.
In 2002, the Millennium Metro Link opened,
tripling the value of every house in the area.
For the first time in its history, Brookfield
was talked of as a 'property hotspot'.

By 2007, a century after the Wainrights
first stepped over the threshold, Number 17
Lawn Lane was a five-bedroom townhouse
with three reception spaces, two bathrooms
and a 60-square-metre (approximately
650-square-foot) open-plan kitchen/dining-
room. The property was valued at more
than $1.5 million.

Extensions have always been an accepted and necessary feature of residential architecture – even John Ruskin, Victorian polymath and purveyor of purity in architectural expression, recognized the need to extend his rural idyll as his needs changed.

2 This studio was one of several additions to Brantwood in the English Lake District, Ruskin's home from 1872 until his death in 1900.

3 Hall'i't'Wood, Bolton, Lancashire, UK, a sixteenth-century timber frame house with a seventeenth-century extension, an indication of increased wealth.

2

3

Social and economic context

If a house is more than 20 years old it is almost certain to have been amended or extended in some way, whether beside, beneath or behind the original. Homes are necessarily flexible. They evolve in tandem with their owners' needs and lifestyles.

Of course this is nothing new, but the early years of the twenty-first century have been a particularly fertile breeding-ground for innovation in the ambition and design of residential extensions. Architects are being challenged as never before. People want to optimize every corner of their homes. In some cases the brief is to create something out of nothing (see Chapter 5, 'Innovative additions'). It is a phenomenon that can be explained by the convergence of a number of economic, political and social trends.

The most significant trend has been the global rise of property prices since the early 1990s, particularly in the major urban centres. Investing in bricks and mortar has never been a decision to take lightly, but aside from the expense, a home offers emotional security and a physical anchor for disparate extended families.

The difference in today's booming market is that the home has also become fundamental to financial security. To many, a well-located, desirable property is a pension plan and the children's inheritance wrapped up into one. Understandably, growing numbers of us are either unwilling to move home, or unable to afford to. The architectural outcome of this domestic stasis is an increased emphasis on improving what we have.

The past decade or so has also seen the revival of city-centre living. In part, this has been driven by government policies on the reuse of urban land in preference to building on precious green fields, although international obligations to reduce carbon emissions have also been a driving force. Tactics for taming car-dependent urban sprawl have been dominating the thoughts of planners in the United States, western Europe and Australia since at least the early 1980s. The outcomes of their thinking are becoming increasingly visible in dense residential rings around city centres, and in the redevelopment of former industrial areas as residential quarters.

4 Kingscote Manor, Newport, USA was one of Rhode Island's earliest summer 'cottages'. Built in the picturesque Gothic Revival style by Richard Upjohn in the 1840s, it was later extended (right of picture) to a design by Stanford White.

5 This Georgian house in Uley, Gloucestershire, UK was extended sideways in the 1920s; a conservatory was added in the 1990s.

4

5

The creative reuse of existing buildings, many of them large industrial structures, has been a steady source of work for architects over the same period. The challenge may have helped to set the tone of innovation now so evident in extensions. The design outcomes – for instance voluminous, clear-spanned rooms divided by flexible partitions with walls of exposed brickwork – have certainly established the generic style template of contemporary urban living.

One of the knock-on effects of increased urban densities is intense demand for the finite number of properties available. Once people have got their hands on a home in one of the newly desirable city centres they are unlikely to let go of it. In fact, there is a greater likelihood of their trying to expand or improve it.

But the popular revival of city-centre living cannot be explained solely by government policies. It also reflects a growing enthusiasm for responsible, twenty-first-century lifestyles. Car ownership is both environmentally damaging and increasingly beyond the means of many. Faced with the choice of living in the suburbs and relying on public transport, or living in the city centre within walking or cycling distance of work and amenities, there is a marked trend towards the latter. And of course the extension of an existing house is so much less demanding on the environment than the construction of a new one.

Another factor in the growing number of housing extensions is that lifestyles are changing. The most obvious shift is in the workplace. Large numbers of us now work from home – if not all the time then certainly some of the time – and that places yet further pressure on space-constricted homes.

But one thing that hasn't changed is the desire for space. Regardless of the socio-economic climate, every home-owner in history has at some stage wondered whether they could add value to their property, or make it a better place to live in if it were larger or better organized. But what is the best way of making sure that your extension is as good as it can be? The simple answer is to use an architect.

Extensions as three-dimensional sculpture: architects have a long history of using extensions as an opportunity to make a statement, whether cultural, personal or playful.

6 The Thematic House, Lansdowne Walk, London, UK (1979–1982). Terry Farrell and clients Charles Jencks and Maggie Keswick collaborated to alter the external grammar of a Victorian terrace house in London's Holland Park. The pair of two-storey interlocking rear conservatories with central spiral staircase and mirrored light shaft was inspired by the cosmos, solar system and changing seasons.

7 House Kada B, Leitnitz, Austria (1996). Klaus Kada transformed the conservative identity of a century-old masonry house by painting it a striking blue/green colour, adding a monolithic plywood extension and linking the two with a double-height glass stairwell.

8 Lescaze House by William Lescaze, 211 E 48th Street, New York, USA (1934). One of the first examples of European functionalism in the USA was an extension that cantilevers out from the front of a New York brownstone. The attention-grabbing counterpoint to its more conventional neighbours was designed to demonstrate that modern architecture could be integrated with existing urban forms.

9 House in Jerusalem, Moshe Safdie, Israel. Safdie's self-designed house is a striking contrast of the ancient and contemporary materials. The brickwork of the ground floor dates to the Crusades; the second floor was added during the Ottoman era. Safdie's curvaceous, glazed addition was completed in 1973.

Why use an architect?

It is easy to question the merit of hiring an architect for an extension, particularly if the solution appears self-explanatory, such as adding a glass-roofed extension to let light into the kitchen. When it is that obvious, what can an architect offer that a builder cannot? The natural conclusion is a do-it-yourself job, but the outcome is almost always a disappointment. What seems an obvious solution very rarely is. To the client, an extension exists in isolation; to an architect, it is part of the whole. Clients are often too close to a building to see the bigger picture and how the addition could impact on adjacent spaces.

An extension can be just as complicated as a new building, if not more so. Aside from the design limitations of working within an existing structure, often on a tight, difficult-to-access site, there are planning, legal and structural issues to take into account.

An architect will consider ventilation, access to light, heating, insulation and structural integrity. He or she will advise on materials, and on the various options for using the space. An architect should also be well connected: many will introduce reliable contractors to the job, meaning that you don't have to find them yourself.

On small residential projects, architects often double as project managers. This means they are responsible for every aspect of the design and construction process, which includes negotiating a way through local planning guidelines, co-ordinating the activities of the various contractors and ensuring that time is not wasted on site. Architects also have professional indemnity insurance, offering legal protection should anything go wrong.

Of course, employing an architect does mean that there is another fee to pay, but in the long run an architect's understanding of space, energy and maintenance costs will save you money. (For advice on how to find an architect and how much to pay see 'Practical considerations', pages 246–248.)

Another reason to employ an architect is that you might engage a star of the future, adding kudos and value – houses with Gehry-designed extensions certainly have a 'unique selling point'. Of course, not everyone achieves fame, but a denominator common to a large majority of small-scale residential projects, be they extensions or interior refurbishments, is that they are the work of young architects.

Before they were famous

Extensions are an opportunity for architects to find their voice and to deal with all the issues of a newbuild without quite the same level of pressure. For many graduates, a residential extension is the first job they ever carry out, which means that they will be thrilled to have the work, desperate to impress and full of ideas germinated during the long process of study. A kitchen extension for an uncle, or a roof-terrace for a family friend is a typical first project. But many are not even that lucky.

7

8

9

In 1956, the first-ever sketch by 14-year-old Tadao Ando was for an extension (unbuilt) to the family home in Japan. He describes it as the moment he realized that 'architecture could be interesting'.

Glenn Murcutt's first job after setting up his own practice in 1969 was a rear extension to his house in Sydney. The addition was a delicate glass pavilion, reminiscent of Mies van der Rohe's Farnsworth House (Plano, Illinois, 1950). The job demonstrates an intimacy with the landscape that has underpinned Murcutt's work ever since. Today he is revered round the world and is widely regarded as Australia's leading architect.

Two of Britain's most celebrated living architects, Norman Foster and Richard Rogers, also started out with an extension. One of the first jobs won by Team 4, a partnership of Foster, Rogers and two sisters, Wendy and Georgie Cheesman (who had all met at Yale University), was a commission to extend the studio of graphic designer FHK Henrion in 1963. Although small, the scheme contains themes that the architects have returned to throughout their careers, in this case using skylights to bring light into deep sections and framing the best of the available views.

Three years later – by which time Foster and Wendy Cheesman had married – Team 4 designed an annexe to Wendy Foster's mother's house in East Horsley, Surrey. The modest suburban extension, which contained an apartment and garage, took the form of five interlocking rectangles in echelon. It may have been a relatively simple brief, but the young architects took the opportunity to try out ideas that they had probably been incubating for years.

Frank Gehry has designed extensions and remodelled private houses throughout his long and illustrious career. One of his first projects was a new kitchen, bedroom and garage for a private house in Los Angeles; the clients were celebrity balladeers Josef Marais and Miranda.

Gehry's sculptural remodelling and extension of his own Santa Monica residence is one of the more renowned residential reinventions of recent years. In two development phases (1977–1978 and

10

1991–1994) the original house, a two-storey 1920s structure clad in pink asbestos shingle with a gambrel roof, was transformed into a collage of different materials and distorted spaces.

Gehry explains: 'We needed some elbow room . . . so I chose to use the five-foot [1.5-metre] front extension, the 14-foot [4.25-metre] side yard extension, and extend six feet [1.8 metres] to the rear to create a one-storey band of space on three sides of the existing house. In other words, I would build a new house around the old house . . .'

The extension was also treated as an opportunity to explore ideas about materials that Gehry was familiar with, notably corrugated steel, plywood and chain-link, and give them new connotations.

It was Gehry's intention that the old and new elements of the building read as 'distinct strong self-sufficient statements, which would gain from each other without compromising themselves'. It is a common balancing act. At some stage the question of whether to mimic the existing structure or to design something demonstrably new crosses the mind of just about every architect working on an extension. In some cases the answer is determined by local

planning guidelines; in others it is down to the discretion of the architect and client to decide what is appropriate.

The phenomenon of young architects graduating from small residential alterations to major public buildings can be brought up to date with the example of Swiss duo Jacques Herzog and Pierre de Meuron. Today they are among the most sought-after architects in the world. Their recent credits include the Tate Modern in London and the Beijing Olympic stadium. But one of their earliest projects, in 1981, was a studio for photographer Rolf Frei-Reimann in Weil-am-Rhein, a German town best known as the home of the Vitra Design Museum. The long, slim extension, which runs the length of Frei-Reimann's back garden, is punctuated by a series of cuboid light-wells in the roof.

Four years later, the nascent superstars designed a private marionette theatre as an addition to a house in Bottmingen, Switzerland. The lightweight timber pavilion, known as the Plywood House, may have been frustratingly low-key for the ambitious pair, but it was an opportunity to grow in confidence and build their portfolio. Everyone has to start somewhere.

10 FHK Henrion studio extension, London, UK (1963). One of the first commissions won by Team 4, the practice established by Norman Foster and Richard Rogers following their return from Yale University, was an extension to the studio of graphic designer FHK Henrion. The architects lowered the existing floor to create a built-in desk; skylights were used to bring light into the deep sections.

11 Studio extension, Weil-am-Rhein, Germany (1981). One of the earliest projects by Herzog & de Meuron was a studio for photographer Rolf Frei-Reimann.

12 Frank Gehry residence, Santa Monica, USA. In 1977 Frank Gehry bought a two-storey gambrel-roofed house covered in pink asbestos shingle. Since then his eclectic alterations and extensions have turned it into one of the most renowned residential reinventions of recent years. The kitchen has been extended and illuminated by a timber-framed glass box balanced at a precarious angle between the perimeter wall and side of the house, allowing the original living room to be expanded and the existing dining room to be converted into a bedroom.

11

12

13 Red Cross House, Jersey Devil, Florida Keys, USA.
   There are cases were the extension overwhelms
   the original. This experimental corrugated steel-
   clad house was built around a small, unpretentious
   seaside cottage. It incorporates living and workspaces,
   and is designed to withstand Florida's sometimes
   extreme weather.

14 Dutra Residence, South Park, California (2003). This
   self-designed extension to the house of architect Jim
   Brown of Public (see also pages 110–115) was built
   to create space for his mother-in-law. On the upper
   level he designed a studio for his wife, a painter. Four
   dwarf citrus trees, moved to accommodate the two-
   storey rear addition, were relocated vertically.

What is a good extension?

Ambition and an enthusiasm for experimentation may be motivational forces for young architects when designing an extension, but to their clients nothing is as relevant as an outcome that improves the liveability, beauty and value of their home.

An over-abundance of architectural 'vision' in small-scale residential alterations can be misplaced and counter-productive. Clients must trust their architects to deliver appropriate solutions; if they don't, what is the point of employing them?

In the context of these potentially oppositional forces, it can be helpful to step back and analyze the characteristics of a 'good' extension.

With such a variety of types and scales, it is difficult to define universal characteristics, but essentially a good extension will revitalize and enrich the existing building in the round, not just the new spaces and the rooms adjacent to them. Even a room in the garden, physically separated from the main house, is part of a broader composition.

Very few of the extensions described in this book – and very few extensions ever built – are stand-alone projects. Most are part of a wider package of renovations and improvements. Even if the client starts out envisaging the work as low-key and small-scale, an architect may not see the challenge in quite the same way.

For instance, to a home-owner a glass-roofed extension to the rear of a property might simply be about enlarging the kitchen and providing more dining space, but to an architect it might be seen as an opportunity to reorganize the entire ground floor, creating a sequence of spaces better suited to a more contemporary way of life. This is not to suggest that architects are always right, but they are almost always worth listening to.

Another positive side-effect of extensions is that they create opportunities to apply contemporary ideas and materials to buildings of different eras. It is easy to forget that houses built in the nineteenth century were designed for an entirely different set of social customs. There may have been a floor for servants' quarters, with small rooms and awkward access. It may also be that perceptions of the neighbourhood have changed over the years: a poor suburban area in the 1880s could well be up-and-coming today. If that is the case it is very likely that the housing stock will be cramped, dark and generally out of keeping with the lifestyle aspirations of its new residents.

But it is not just historic buildings that can be improved with the addition of an extension. More recent buildings can also benefit – whatever architects may say, they rarely get everything right the first time around. Circulation, access, ventilation, natural light and internal decorations can all be enhanced. All it takes is some careful thinking.

15 Bungalow Pop-up Addition, Olson Sundberg Kundig Allen Architects, Seattle, USA (2000). 'We love the area, but we need more space,' is one of the most common reasons for building an extension, as was the case at this family home in Seattle.

16 'Internal' extension, Cassandra Fahey, Melbourne, Australia (2004). Not all buildings can be extended externally. Faced with the challenge of creating space within a heritage-protected building, architect Cassandra Fahey designed a lantern-like sculptural addition to enclose a bedroom, study area, bathroom and staircase to the new roof terrace.

16

About this book

No two clients have exactly the same ambitions. The most common reasons for needing more space are a growing family and working from home. But needs vary enormously. At different times of life people may need separate accommodation for an elderly parent or nanny, or a roof-terrace. Others may wish to reclaim a cherished view obscured by a new high-rise development, or to build an extension as a way of making their home more environmentally sustainable.

By the same token, no two properties are identical. In some cases there may be only one way to extend. The most common directions are up – adding another storey, a roof-terrace or a penthouse on top of a high-rise – and behind – typically building a ground-level rear extension to connect the kitchen with the garden. But there are numerous other options.

This book describes 39 architect-designed extensions to private homes in 12 countries around the world. Each example outlines the client's requirements and the

architect's solution, as well as the major hurdles and challenges encountered during the design and build process.

The case studies are arranged around five chapters, each dedicated to different types of extension. The first four, 'Up & under', 'Back & front', 'Sideways' and 'Outdoors', are self-explanatory. The final chapter focuses on what to do when no other options are available. It's about innovation and invention, two of the enduring characteristics of successful design in any context.

Up & under

1

1 The timber-clad bedroom wings cantilever out over the back garden, projecting a sense of dynamic modernity entirely at odds with the street-facing façade.

2 The house dates from the 1880s. It is a survivor of Melbourne's post-Gold-Rush property boom.

Armadale House

Melbourne | Australia | Jackson Clements Burrows Architects | Space added: 240m² (2,580ft²)

The front half of the Holkners' house dates from the 1880s. It is one of the last original post-Gold-Rush-era properties in the wide leafy street. The grey-painted masonry façade is composed of two pitched-roof side sections linked by a covered veranda. It is solid, unpretentious and unassuming.

The back of the house is something else altogether. Two long timber-clad wings cantilever out over the garden. They are cuboids, with flat roofs and large windows. The effect is theatrical and striking.

Jodie Holkner and her husband Mark, a successful manufacturer of tissue and toilet paper, moved to the affluent Melbourne suburb of Armadale in 1995. 'An extension had been tacked onto the back of the house in the 1980s,' says Jodie Holkner. 'It was half underground, and felt a bit like a dungeon. The children's bedrooms were down there.' The decision to get rid of this extension and rearrange the house was made shortly before Jodie became pregnant with the couple's fourth daughter.

Jackson Clements Burrows Architects were recommended to Jodie by a sister-in-law. Their initial design sketch was close to what the Holkners had in mind. The brief was to add a second level to the house, with five bedrooms, all with en suite bathrooms. Downstairs the challenge was to reconfigure the living spaces, create a platform to show off the family's contemporary art collection, and reconnect the house with the garden.

2

3 The upper-level extension reinforces and accentuates the U-shaped form of the original rear courtyard. At ground level the aim was to reconnect the house with the garden.

JCB's approach was based on reviving the original U-shaped Victorian floor plan, which enclosed a small paved area at the rear, elevated slightly above the garden. The addition of the second level, following the outline of the perimeter walls, was planned to reinforce this configuration. The cantilevered bedroom wings, clad in vertical strips of western red cedar, were designed to re-establish the connection between the house and outdoor spaces; the southern wing extends 4.5 metres (14 feet 9 inches) into the garden.

Tim Jackson was the project architect: 'It was like an editing job. We were cutting and pasting old and new elements to create a liveable family home.'

Internally, the process of integrating the various elements – old and new; upstairs and downstairs – is assisted by the floor plan, with the two wings separated by a distinct central section. At ground level, the southern wing is a large, light-filled linear kitchen. The northern wing encloses a spacious lounge, an office for Jodie and Mark, and a fish tank built into the internal wall. The central connecting space is used as a formal dining-room.

On the upper level, the southern wing is dedicated to the children's bedrooms. The master bedroom with attached dressing-room occupies the northern wing. At the top of the staircase, above the dining-room, is a play-space for the children.

The work took six months to design and 15 to build. The Holkners moved back into their house at the end of 2003.

3

4 The central entrance lobby acts as both a circulation hub and a canvas for the Holkners' extensive collection of contemporary art.

5 The remodelled kitchen and dining wing reaches into the garden. At the eastern end, full-height doors offer onto an outdoor dining area.

6 Upper-level floor plan

7 Ground-level floor plan

8 Cross-section looking south

9 Cross-section looking north

'It was like an editing job. We were cutting and pasting old and new elements to create a liveable family home'

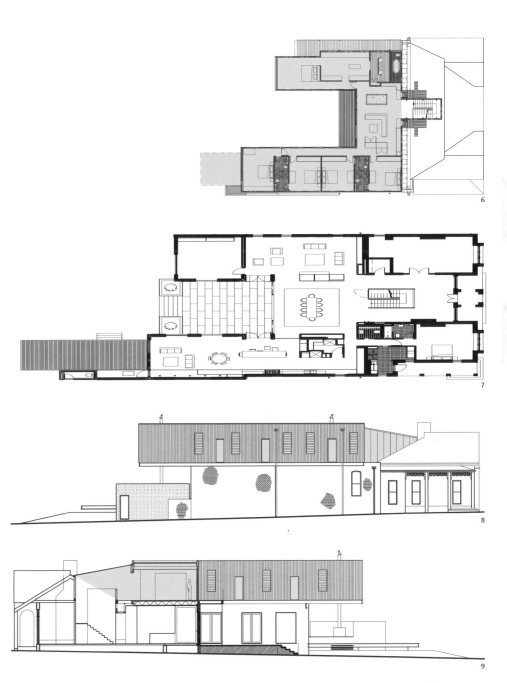

1

1 The existing footprint was unusually wide at 9 metres (30 feet), a legacy of the structure's original incarnation as a commercial workshop or garage.

2 In 1960, the building and much of the surrounding area were severely damaged by a jet turbine that fell from an airliner.

Brooklyn house

New York | USA | Baumann Architecture | Space added: 93m² (1,000ft²)

Number 77 Prospect Place in Brooklyn began life in the late nineteenth century and according to the owner, Noel Wiggins, it had probably been a commercial workshop or garage.

Some time in the early twentieth century it became a shop; its 9-metre (30-foot) street-facing frontage was adorned with an ornate cast-iron façade. Things took a turn for the worse in 1960 when a jet turbine from an airliner crashed through the roof.

The 1970s saw a revival, when it was among a number of buildings restored by a gas utilities company eager to kick-start the gentrification of what was then a rather rough neighbourhood. Since then the house has been through a number of residential incarnations, most recently as home to a Hollywood screenwriter.

When the present owners bought the property in 2002, the building was in good condition. The interior was Modernist in style, with a large skylight in the roof; Wiggins believes that the gas company carried out this work, as well as adding the basement. The only thing missing was space.

'That's why we decided to add another floor,' explains Wiggins. 'But while we wanted more space, we didn't want it to feel like an industrial loft. We prefer softer, natural materials.' Old friend Philippe Baumann was called in for design advice.

3 Street-facing elevation

4 A small black steel balcony lends presence to the
façade of the new upper-level addition.

At the outset the challenge was to add another level on top of the building, but as things evolved the two existing levels were also altered. The work took two years, and the original budget of $300,000 eventually rose to $1.5 million. 'I just kept chasing the dream,' says Wiggins, who runs a design and importing company. 'But it's beautifully designed and works really well.'

The first phase of construction involved pouring a continuous concrete bond beam on top of the existing parapet wall to level it out in preparation for the addition of the second floor, a 93-square-metre (1,000-square-foot) steel-framed loft space. The steel-beamed ceiling of the ground-level space is original. The second floor was added with minimal disturbance to the original roof.

Letting light in was a key feature of the job. To allow light into the ground floor the position of the steel-framed addition was offset by 0.9 metres (3 feet), creating an 11-metre (36-foot) light-well in the living space below. Several other openings were made, notably on the new storey, where wrap-around clerestories and plate-glass north and south façades allow light to flood in. 'One bemused carpenter said: "It's like being outside,"' says Baumann.

Emphasis was also placed on articulating the nature of the materials. Various timbers, recycled bricks, concrete and cast-iron columns were all left exposed and untreated, to maximize the sense of warmth and harmony with nature. Organic lime-wash pigments were used throughout, to accentuate the natural irregularities of the walls.

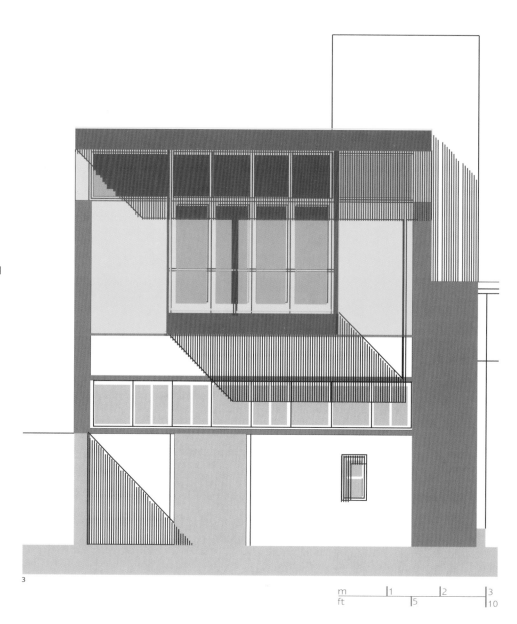

3

m |1 |2 |3
ft |5 |10

5 To allow light into the ground level the floor of the second storey was offset by 0.9 metres (3 feet), creating a light-well 11 metres (36 feet) long.

6 Planting and extensive use of glazing help to connect internal and external areas.

7 The timber, lime-wash and cast-iron columns were left exposed and untreated to maximize the natural qualities of the materials.

6

5

The family – which includes two young boys – uses the upper storey as a multi-purpose space for special events and relaxation. Sliding walls and three-quarter-height partitions make it open and flexible.

The remodelled ground floor contains the main living spaces, including three bedrooms, two bathrooms, a large kitchen and a living-room. The basement contains the library, an office and storage space.

7

Wrap-around clerestories and plate-glass
north and south façades allow light to flood in.
One bemused carpenter said,
'It's like being outside'

1

1 Instead of replicating the footprint of the existing building, the extension projects over the edge, creating a distinctive marker at the corner of the two streets. It is also slightly shorter, to allow room for a rear balcony.

2 The trapezoidal steel-framed box is clad in sheets of black-painted aluminum; it took only a morning to lift into place.

Furniture maker's bedroom

Lille | France | Isabelle Menu and Luc Saison | Space added: 77m² (829ft²)

The owner of this small four-storey redbrick house is a furniture maker, and he and his wife bought the property as a home for their young family. The trouble was that the traditional Flemish-style terrace was too small for their needs, and they had limited funds to extend the house: a quandary familiar to millions.

When architects Isabelle Menu and Luc Saison first visited the house they judged it to be of limited quality, and with little potential for improvement. The challenge was exacerbated by the building's prominent location on a corner plot in Lille. The only available ground-level space, a long garden, was both prohibitively narrow and out of the question because of planning constraints. None of this was helping the owners, who needed space – and they needed it quickly.

Menu and Saison judged that with some persuasion they could convince the planning authorities to accept a rooftop extension, particularly if it reinforced the form of the corner. They also recognized that costs could be minimized if the extension was manufactured off-site rather than in situ.

The existing pitched roof was removed and the walls were reinforced. The lightweight steel-framed trapezoidal box was then lifted into place by crane, the process taking only a morning to complete.

Instead of sitting directly on top of the external walls, the box is slightly offset. It

2

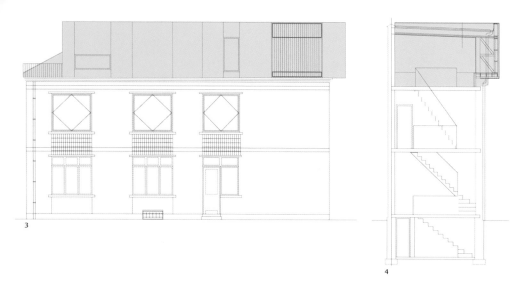

3

4

5

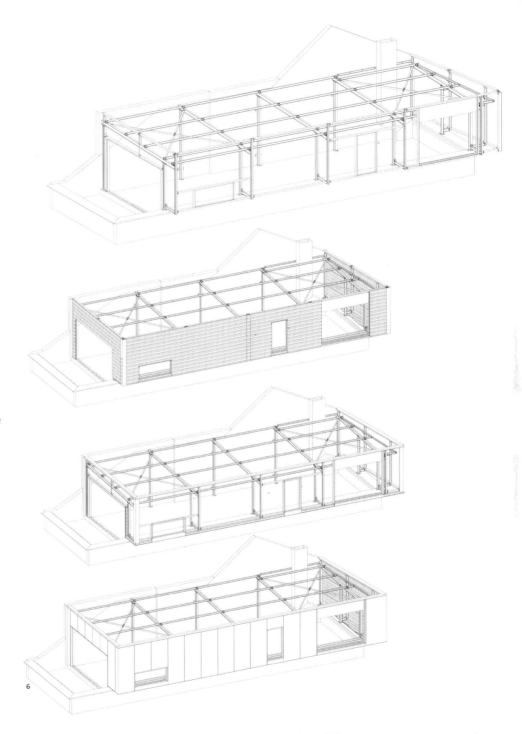

3 Elevation of long street-facing façade

4 Cross-section

5 The rooftop box projects from the side of the building, creating a distinctive urban feature on the corner site.

6 The extension was manufactured off-site and lifted into place by crane, reducing costs substantially.

projects 80 centimetres (2 feet 8 inches) over the edge of the walls, and is slightly shorter than the building's footprint, creating space for a small balcony at the rear.

The large open-plan area is used as the parents' bedroom and living space. As well as access to the roof-terrace, it includes built-in storage and a full-height picture window. A staircase which previously offered access to the low storage space leads from the floor below. The 5.5-metre-by-14-metre (18-foot-by-46-foot) structure increases the liveable area of the house by about a third.

On the lower levels, Menu and Saison removed as many partition walls as was viable, to open up the space and let light flood in: a cheap and effective tactic for creating a flexible house suited to the needs of a twenty-first-century family.

On all levels, the furnishings and fittings were designed by the client, which helps to explain the low cost of €30,000 ($37,500). The entire process – from design to completion – took three months.

6

It was a cheap and effective tactic for creating a flexible house suited to the needs of a twenty-first-century family

1

2

3

1 The original pitched-roof three-storey apartment block was built in 1958.

2 As well as the addition of the penthouse, the exterior of the building was given a face-lift, with a dark grey mineral-based plaster replacing the original stucco.

3 The penthouse projects a sense of pure, luxurious, glazed Modernity.

Lightweight penthouse

Stuttgart | Germany | Hartwig N. Schneider Architekten | Space added: penthouse 145m² (1,560ft²); roof-terrace 102m² (1,100ft²)

This delicate, lightweight penthouse is the home of architect couple Gabriele and Professor Hartwig N. Schneider, who designed it as part of a comprehensive renovation and expansion of a three-storey apartment block.

The original structure, perched on the side of a hill overlooking Stuttgart, where the forest gives way to vineyards, dates from the late 1950s. It was built as a serviced apartment block; many of the original residents were local railway workers. Like so much housing in post-Second-World-War Europe, it was built quickly and cheaply, so by 1994, when the building was bought by Gabriele Schneider, it was showing signs of age.

Initially the Schneiders used the top floor as their office and rented out the lower-level apartments. They made running repairs, including putting in new window-frames and replacing the original stucco with a dark grey mineral-based plaster. But it wasn't until 2001 that they decided to take serious action, restoring all the apartments, fitting out the top level as an open-plan office for their practice, and building a penthouse on the roof.

The structural limitations of the existing building, and local planning guidelines determined the scale of the penthouse, its position on the roof and the materials used.

In planning terms, the penthouse is a Dachgeschoss (attic), for which the

4

4 From its position on the side of a valley, the penthouse commands views of Stuttgart and surrounding vineyards.

5 Rear elevation

6 Floor plan of the apartment: the large roof-terrace is a product of planning regulations which require that the enclosed area of the apartment be only 70 per cent of the floor below.

requirement is that its built area should cover no more than 70 per cent of the floor below. This led to the L-shaped apartment and the large roof-terrace.

The penthouse is extremely light, and minimal almost to the point of invisibility. At first glance it projects an almost Farnsworth House sense of luxurious, ordered, glazed Modernity.

It is built around a slim frame of galvanized steel. Full-height glass walls enclose the volume, including six sliding doors, each 1.9 metres (6 feet 2 inches) wide, that sit in frames of untreated aluminium, allowing access to the timber-decked terrace and encouraging cross-ventilation.

During the hot summer months sunscreens are used to mimimize heat gain; double-glazed insulated glass helps to retain heat during the winter. The roof of the penthouse is made of trapezoidal corrugated-metal sheets, which span more than 6 metres (19 feet 6 inches).

An external spiral staircase offers access to the penthouse, which is also linked to the office floor. The two lower levels, which include Hartwig N. Schneider Architekten's model workshop, a communal kitchen, a meeting-room and eight one-bedroom apartments, are accessed via the main internal staircase.

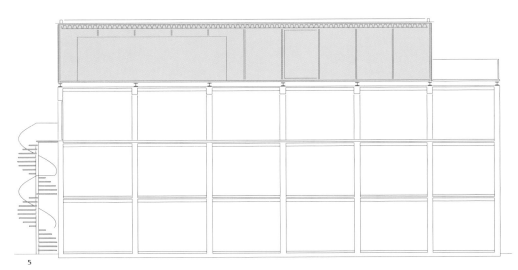

5

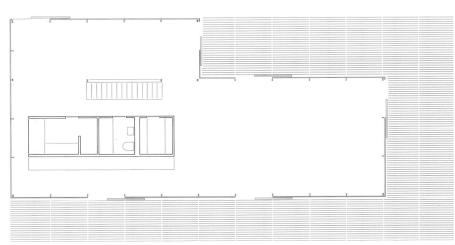

6

7 Full-height glass walls and sliding doors enclose the slim galvanized steel frame.

8 The galley kitchen.

9 Sliding doors encourage cross-ventilation. During winter the double-glazed insulated glass retains heat.

The structural limitations of the existing building, and local planning guidelines determined the scale of the penthouse, its position on the rooftop and the choice of materials

1

1 Full-height sliding doors offer access to the terrace, from which the Hudson River is visible to the south-west.

2 The original two-storey house was built in 1820. A third storey was added later. Over the years the building has been used as industrial premises and divided into apartments.

3 For privacy and protection from the elements, the open-air terrace in front of the penthouse can be closed off behind screens.

Photographer's penthouse

New York | USA | Christoff:Finio Architecture | Space added: 46m² (500ft²)

2

3

Photographer Jan Staller loved his view of the Hudson River: the wide expanse of dark blue water was visible to the north-west from the third floor of his house in New York's West Village. That was all jeopardized, however, when plans for three 16-storey residential towers designed by Richard Meier were unveiled for sites on nearby Perry Street. When complete, the new buildings would eclipse that cherished aspect.

When Staller approached architect Martin Finio, he had a simple request: to reclaim his view of the Hudson. The solution was the addition of a new level on the roof, capturing views of the river to the south-west.

As with so many urban buildings over a certain age, this is not the first time that the property has been extended. It was built in 1820 as a two-storey house. Since then a third storey was added, it was adapted for industrial use, and it was divided into apartments. When Staller bought the building in 1992, he converted it back into a single house. Building a fourth storey, however, was uncharted territory. The roof, which sloped from front to back, had never previously been built on.

Two of the challenges facing the architects were to optimize the roof space while conforming to planning regulations, and to ensure a sense of privacy from the industrial buildings on the opposite side of the street.

4 Owner Jan Staller uses the small, light-filled penthouse as a space for relaxation.

5 Cross-section looking south-west.

6 Floor plan: planning regulations stipulated that the floor area of the penthouse must not occupy more than 33 per cent of the building's footprint.

Regulations stated that the total height of the building, including the extension, must not be higher than the width of the facing street. They also stated that the total floor area of the addition must not exceed 33 per cent of the building's footprint. This is the reason for the open-air terrace at the front of the penthouse; the flexible outdoor space can be enclosed by screens that cover the roof and sides, thereby adhering to the regulations and affording privacy.

The steel-framed penthouse was built in situ. Its walls are insulated with a layer of high-density extruded polystyrene foam filled in with cast concrete (ARXX system), 15 centimetres (6 inches) thick. The exterior finish is synthetic stucco.

Access from the third storey to the penthouse is via an elegant metal staircase which was designed by Staller.

4

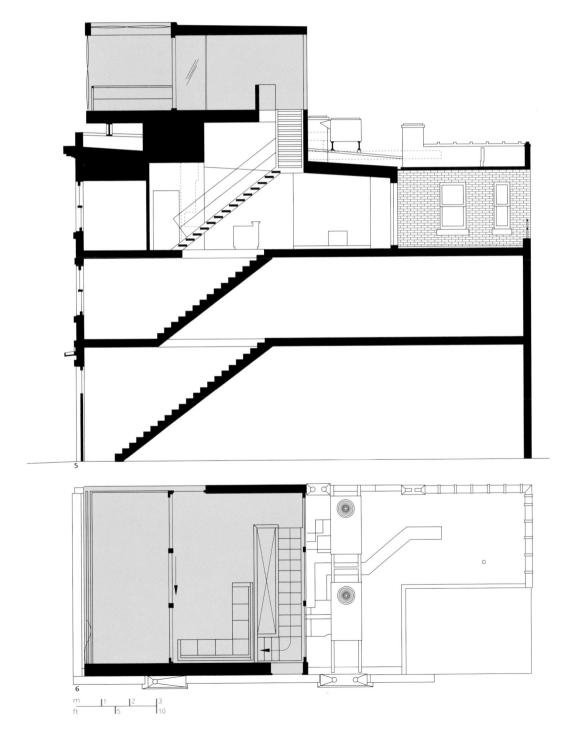

m |1 |2 |3
ft |5 |10

7 The kitchen in the third-storey living area.

8 Staller designed the elegant metal staircase that links
the third storey to the penthouse.

The challenge was to optimize the roof space while conforming to planning regulations, and ensuring a sense of privacy from the industrial buildings opposite

1

1 The penthouse apartment sits on top of a 1960s office block in the centre of Vienna. It is the 'missing link' between the gable lines of two neighbouring buildings.

2 Sheets of aluminium-clad plastic enclose the steel frame, creating an expressive and highly sculptural effect.

House Ray 1

Vienna | Austria | Delugan Meissl Associated Architects | Space added: 230m² (2,476ft²)

Externally angular like a stealth bomber, internally fluid like a luxury liner, this structurally innovative penthouse is imaginative, beautifully detailed and Bond-set stylish. It could only be the home of an architect, in this instance Roman Delugan and Elke Delugan-Meissl, who designed it for themselves and their young family.

House Ray 1 – the name is a reference to the couple's daughter, Nora Ray Delugan – sits on top of a six-storey 1960s office block in Vienna's fourth district. It is the 'missing link' between the gable lines of two neighbouring buildings, a factor that determined the height and influenced the form of the rooftop extension.

Perhaps unsurprisingly, given the prominence of the location and the extremely unusual design, the process of securing planning consent was not straightforward. The architects invoked Paragraph 69, local legislation which accommodates enlightened analysis of particularly innovative designs that will impact on the city's skyline; the clause was also used by Hans Hollein in the 1980s to secure consent for the Haas Haus, a heavily glazed commercial building opposite St Stephen's Cathedral, also in Vienna.

To spread the load evenly over the 340-square-metre (3,660-square-foot) rooftop, the penthouse is built around a steel skeleton, the bearing-points of which are positioned on the columns of

Angular like a stealth bomber, and fluid like a luxury liner, this structurally innovative penthouse is imaginative, beautifully detailed and Bond-set stylish

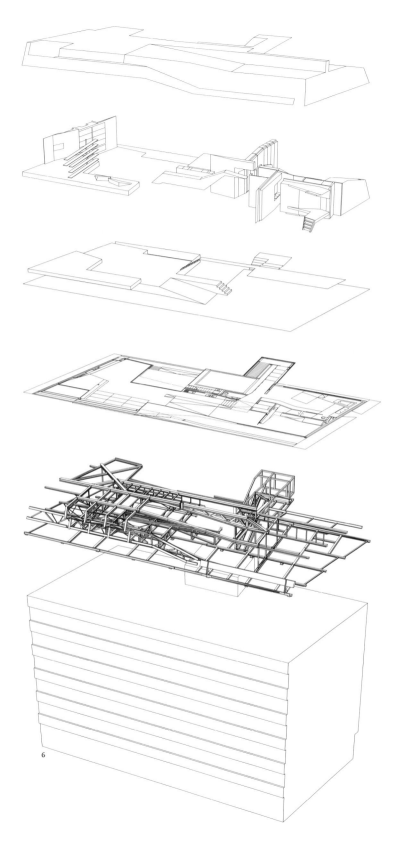

3 The bath, like almost all fittings and furniture throughout the apartment, is integrated into the steel frame.

4 Access from the top of the office lift-shaft to the apartment is via a staircase enclosed within a box that cantilevers out from the rear of the building.

5 The steel frame facilitates a column-free open-plan interior, with the means of support hidden behind MDF and acrylic panels.

6 The steel frame was constructed off-site and lifted into place by crane. To spread the load, the bearing points of the steel frame sit on the columns of the office building.

the office building below. It is this frame that facilitates the expressive sculptural forms and the open-plan column-free internal arrangement, or the 'flowing spatial continuum', as the architects put it.

Subtle changes in floor height are used to define different functions. For instance, the large living space and central kitchen are about a metre (3 feet) below the bedrooms, making the bedrooms feel more intimate and protected.

The open kitchen, located on a 'plateau' at the bottom of a shallow incline leading up to the living area, has been designed as the hub around which the apartment pivots.

The most dramatic feature is a leather-upholstered seating area that cantilevers out beyond the roofline of the office block on the rear façade. The lounge, like the rest of the structure, is supported on the steel skeleton; this enabled the architects to make expansive use of structural glass to optimize the views of the city.

The steel frame also supports built-in furniture and fittings, including the beds, baths, closets and kitchen fittings. The kitchen table and chairs are among the few pieces of furniture that are not integrated into the design.

There are external terraces on both sides of the apartment, one with a small swimming pool, adding to the sense of innovation and opulence.

Access to the rooftop apartment is via a staircase enclosed within a box that cantilevers out from the rear of the building. The staircase is at the top of the lift-shaft which extends to the fifth floor.

7

7 Previous pages: Panoramic views of Vienna are visible from the dining area and the enclosed courtyard with integrated lap pool.

8 Floor plan

9 A small swimming pool is built into one of the external terraces, helping to minimize the apartment's visual impact from street level.

10 A 'relaxation zone' with leather-upholstered seating cantilevers out from the rear of the building, optimizing views of Vienna.

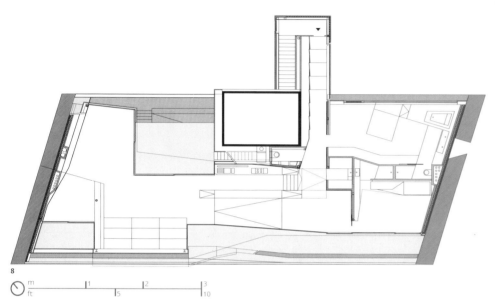

8

m
ft
|1
|5
|2
|3
|10

9

The challenge was complicated by two factors: the
relatively poor quality of the original house, and strict
planning regulations

1 The rooftop bedroom extension and a comprehensive internal reorganization have helped to unite three previously disconnected volumes.

2 The flat-roofed, four-storey timber-and-stucco townhouse bears little resemblance to the original ivy-covered structure.

Rooftop bedrooms

Montrouge | France | Tectône | Space added: 60m² (646ft²)

This was more than an extension: not only did the addition of a fourth storey to a handsome but spatially discordant pitched-roof townhouse give the building a new identity and a fresh lease of life, but the flat-roofed, timber-and-stucco-finished outcome bears almost no similarity to the original building.

Montrouge is a suburb directly south of Paris. It has grown rapidly in recent years, but there are still a few pockets of older properties to be found. This house, on avenue Jean-Jaurès, is in one of them; it dates from the early 1900s and occupies a triangular plot with front and back gardens.

Architects Pascal Chombart de Lauwe and Sabri Bendimérad of Tectône were commissioned to renovate the structure and double the number of bedrooms from three to six. The challenge was complicated by two factors: the relatively poor quality of the original house, and strict planning regulations. The existing surface area of the house, 230 square metres (2,476 square feet), could only be extended by 60 square metres (646 square feet).

The architects' solution was to strip out the existing building, allowing them to completely rearrange the living spaces and add a new third storey to house the bedrooms and a bathroom.

The removal of the pitched roof revealed structural imperfections in the external walls, which meant that the extension

2

3 A staircase suspended on steel cables from a crossbeam in the roof unites the previously disparate volumes and allows light to flood the interior.

4 The flat roof projects out to protect the plywood walls and shutters of the rooftop timber extension.

5 Shutters closed

6 Following the removal of the pitched roof the walls of the house were strengthened prior to the addition of the lightweight timber-framed extension.

7 The architects describe the new level as 'a piece of fine furniture sitting on top of the existing structure'.

would need to be lightweight. Bendimérad and Chombart de Lauwe decided to treat the timber-framed addition as 'a piece of fine furniture sitting on top of the existing structure'. Its polished appearance belies its simplicity and unpretentious components: it is an insulated box clad in thick plywood.

The plywood cladding extends down the left-hand side of the street-facing façade, enclosing a small rooftop addition to two previously disconnected brick-built structures projecting at 90 degrees from the main house. For the first time, the two side buildings have been properly integrated into the house. The cladding is an external expression of this alteration. It also contrasts with the white stucco of the original brick structure, reinforcing the distinctions between old and new, both technically and materially.

Internally the potentially jarring interaction between the new and old elements is addressed by a new staircase suspended on steel cables from the cross-beam of the flat roof. This provides a dramatic and stylish central point to the unified family home.

The work cost €277,000 ($350,000) and took nine months to complete, but there may still be room for growth. Planning regulations notwithstanding, the clients identified the garage as the site for the next extension. A second- and even a third-storey addition would certainly reinforce the 'corner' composition of the street-facing façade. In the meantime, Montrouge is getting used to the altered image of one of its older relics.

3

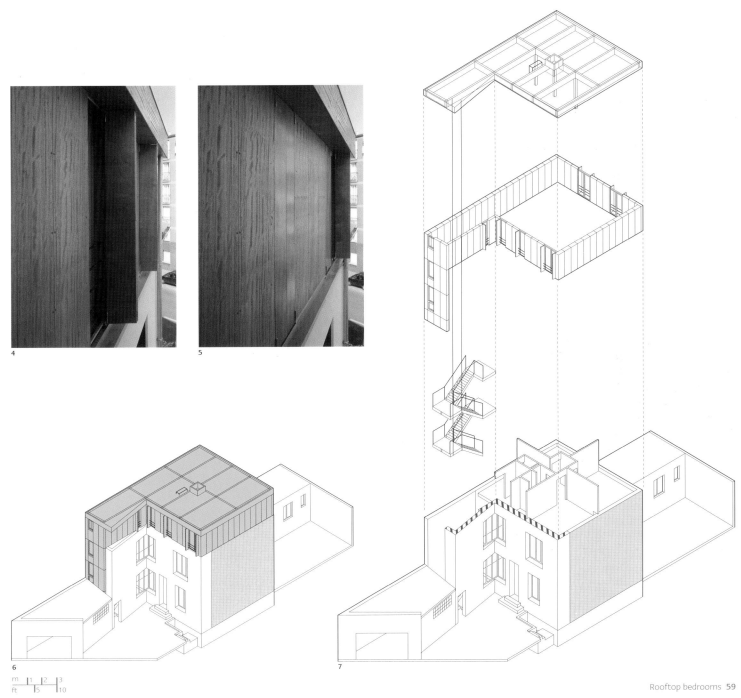

4

5

6

7

m |1 |2 |3
ft |5 |10

1

1 The multi-purpose subterranean entertainment and relaxation space includes a gym, bathroom, hot tub and home cinema.

2 A swimming pool was originally planned for the 9-metre-deep (30-foot-deep) void. The idea was rejected following objections from neighbours.

3 The basement is hidden away underneath the back garden of a nineteenth-century mid-terrace townhouse.

Underground entertainment space

London | UK | Granit Chartered Architects | Space added: 70m² (753ft²)

This deluxe multi-purpose playroom beneath a west London garden was originally planned as a swimming pool. The change of use was enforced by the local planning authority, which had received objections from neighbours concerned that the pool would be too noisy and would emit noxious chlorine fumes.

By the time the negative decision came through the excavation work was almost complete, so the cavernous void – 14 metres (46 feet) long, 5 metres (16 feet 5 inches) wide and 9 metres (30 feet) below ground – was fitted out with a cinema, gym, hot tub and massage area instead.

Not everyone can afford to extend underground. It can also be a complex and messy challenge, often requiring a building to be underpinned, and finding ways to get large construction equipment beneath the property. There may also be concerns about subsidence, and the structural impact on adjacent properties.

In this case money was no obstacle. The basement was part of a £500,000 ($900,000) refurbishment of a five-bedroom house in one of London's more prestigious residential areas.

The first challenge was to get a truck and a nine-metre drilling machine into the back garden of a nineteenth-century mid-terrace townhouse. This required the removal of the external ground-floor walls, to enable the truck to be driven under the

2

3

house. The drill was dismantled and taken through piece by piece.

With the equipment in place, the excavation could begin. Around six months later, and with the planning dispute settled, the space was ready to be fitted out. Robert Wilson of Granit describes the challenge as 'Designing an urban subterranean retreat with a sense of fun ... Soho bar meets industrial bunker. It's pure indulgence.'

The basement is entered through the kitchen extension at the back of the house. A shallow mezzanine leads to a large open-plan void via a staircase with rough-hewn oak treads. At the far end of the room is a hot tub, exposed to the elements by a full-height shaft. When not in use the tub can be closed off by a sliding door which doubles as a projection screen for films. Underneath the mezzanine the architects found space for a shower-room, a sauna and a gym.

Although the basement is deep, natural light floods it, principally from the floor-to-ceiling window on the mezzanine level.

A new landscaped garden sits on top of the structure. It is a simple, low-maintenance space, consisting of water rills, planting areas and teak benches. Few visitors would be able to guess what they were sitting on top of.

4

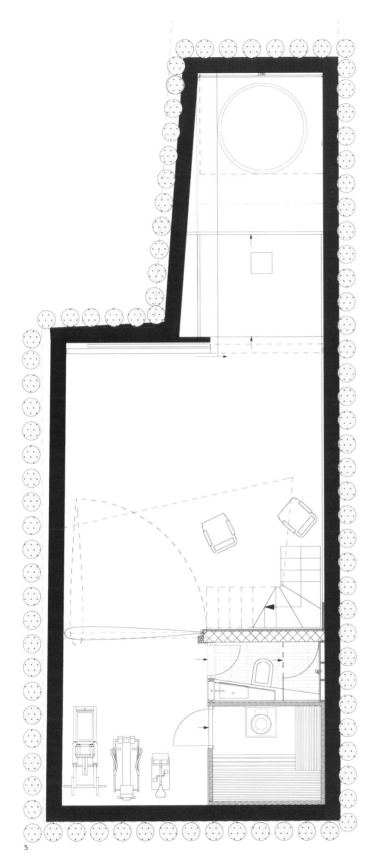

5

7 Sliding screens and folding doors can be arranged to turn the basement into a private cinema or open-plan party space.

1

1 The boxy body of the house contrasts with the barrel-vaulted hull-like roof, a reference to the maritime heritage of Moss Beach.

2 The original two-bedroom bungalow.

3 As well as adding another level, the remodel included extending the footprint to the rear and taking a slice out of the garage.

Vermont Avenue House

Moss Beach | California | USA | Aidlin Darling Design | Space added: 102m² (1,100ft²)

Erik and Tena Watts moved to Moss Beach in 1991, just before a property boom hit the Californian seaside town. By 1998, when the couple were expecting their second child, new developments and large-scale refurbishments were sprouting up all around their two-bedroom bungalow.

The Wattses' much-loved ocean views and sense of privacy were under threat, and with space soon to become even tighter than it already was, they were faced with a quandary: to move, or to extend.

They were reluctant to take the former option, as the location, just two blocks from the sea-front, suited them perfectly. Instead, they asked an architect friend, David Darling, to consider the options for expansion. Budgetary considerations were paramount; the Wattses did not want to pay much more than the cost of moving.

Working closely together, Darling and his clients managed to shave approximately 20 per cent off the standard cost for a residential extension in the San Francisco Bay area. A range of cost-cutting tactics was applied. For instance, the Wattses took a hands-on approach to the work and as far as possible selected tradespeople whom they knew and trusted, many of whom charged them substantially less than their typical rates. Client and architect also sourced mass-produced components and designed around a standard four-foot module, thereby minimizing labour costs.

2

3

The Wattses' ocean views and privacy were under threat . . . they were faced with a quandary: to move, or to extend.

4 The new upper-storey balcony optimizes the expansive green views to the south. On the ground level, glass doors and a full-height window allow light into the family room.

5 Untreated cedar cladding on the rear and west façades and the new upper storey creates a distinctive and homogenous two-storey house.

There were three aspects to the brief: to create more space, draw natural light inside the building, and orientate the house away from neighbouring properties. The solution was to add a second level, extend the building footprint into the rear and side yards, and take a slice out of the internal garage. The work also involved a comprehensive reorganization of the existing ground floor.

In the house's original configuration the two bedrooms were at the rear of the property, next to a small bathroom. Today those bedrooms have been converted into a large family room that reaches out into the back garden; full-height glass doors and a window 2.4 metres by 2.4 metres (8 feet by 8 feet) allow light to flood in. The bathroom has been built into the garage, next to the children's bedrooms.

The new open-plan upper level contains a sequence of flexible zones for sleeping, dressing, bathing and working. The south-facing balcony and clerestory windows make it feel light and airy.

For the hull-like barrel-vaulted roof, Darling and his clients specified Alaskan yellow cedar, a weather-resistant timber that is well suited to the coastal conditions. On the interior, laminated beams resemble the ribs of a boat frame.

The exterior has also been overhauled to create a homogenous entity as opposed to an external articulation of new and old elements. Strips of untreated cedar clad the rear and west façades and the new upper storey. The material is water- and insect-resistant, although it needs to be bleached every five years or so to counteract mould.

4

5

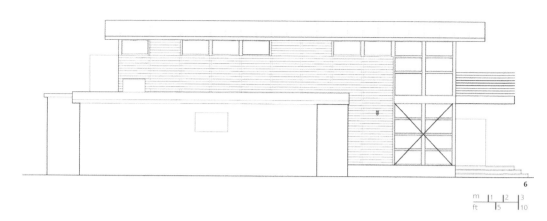

6

6 West elevation

7 The new upper level includes an office, master bedroom and bathroom.

8 Exposed beams and walls of gypsum plaster create a spare, modern, semi-industrial atmosphere.

9 South elevation

8

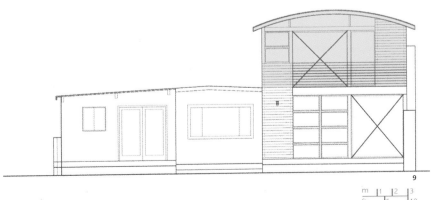

9

m |1 |2 |3
ft |5 |10

1

1 The roof of the subterranean extension forms a terrace and garden in front of the children's bedrooms on the first floor.

2 The original nineteenth-century alpine villa, which was partially derelict when bought, has protected views over Lake Bled.

Villa at Lake Bled

Slovenia | Ofis Arhitekti | Space added: approximately 600m² (6,500ft²)

Lake Bled is one of Slovenia's most picturesque and exclusive alpine resorts and has long been home to the great and good of society. Former Yugoslav leader Tito, who was Slovene on his mother's side, had a villa there which is now one of several luxury hotels with lake views. Bled has the added benefit of being only an hour's drive from the capital, Ljubljana, meaning that it falls within the commuter belt.

It was this rare combination of social and geographic conditions that in 2002 prompted a Ljubljana-based lawyer to buy a partially derelict villa overlooking the lake. His plan was to relocate his family to the alpine idyll.

Several architects were invited to propose ideas for the renovation and extension of the nineteenth-century villa. Based on the recommendation of a friend Ofis Arhitekti, led by Rok Oman and Špela Videčnik, was selected for the job.

It was a prescient decision: Ofis is now regarded as among Europe's most promising architecture studios. The subterranean extension was among its first commissions.

The challenge was to create a spacious extension that could not be seen from the lake – planning regulations demand that every building and tree visible from the lake be preserved.

Oman and Videčnik's solution was to gut the villa, lower the ground around it by a

2

3 The graceful exposed timber staircase ascends gently through the building from the basement living areas to the upper levels.

4 Cross-section illustrating the role of the staircase in connecting the old and new parts of the building.

5 The architects describe the basement as a 'pillow under the villa'. It effectively doubles the liveable floor space.

storey, wrap new living spaces around the exposed base and insert a staircase through a central void to the existing building above. The architects describe the extension as a 'pillow under the villa'. It effectively doubles the size of the house.

Ofis Arhitekti used materials and structural composition to emphasize the distinction between the new and old parts of the building. The rounded forms of the extension appear to coil around the central staircase, a serpentine yin to the rigid yang of the formal nineteenth-century architecture above; the plain walls and gabled bays of the existing structure are a stark contrast with the glass and dark iroko finishes of the curvaceous addition.

The luxurious timber-lined interior walls of the extension are all visible from the staircase. The simplicity of the space, enriched by discreet shifts of floor level and generous windows, creates a contemporary twist on the Bled tradition of aristocratic grandeur.

To shield views of the entry façade, soil excavated from underneath the building has been used to form a narrow ledge; semi-mature trees minimize views of the house from the lake.

Completion of the extension was originally projected to take a little more than a year, but a serious fire halfway through the project conspired against that time-frame. The upside to the story is that the 'old' villa visible today is a replica that is much more solid than the original.

3

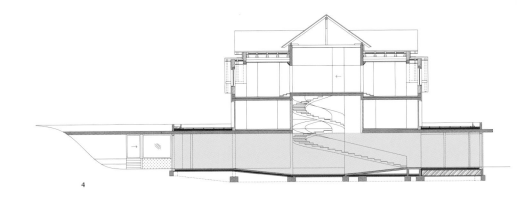

4

5

The challenge was
to create a spacious
extension that could
not be seen from
the lake

6 Floor plan of the basement extension

7 Ground-floor plan

8 First-floor plan

9 The soft rounded forms of the basement extension appear to coil around the staircase, a serpentine yin to the rigid yang of the formal nineteenth-century architecture above.

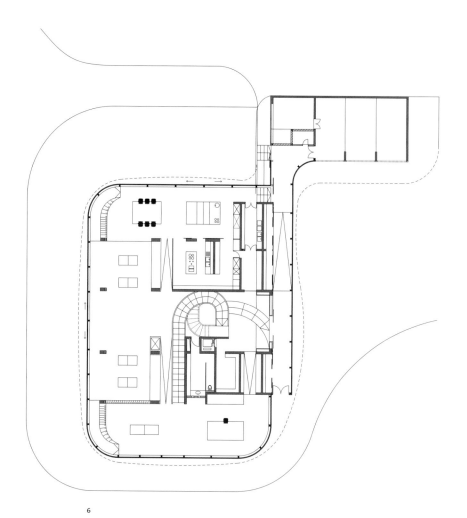

6

9

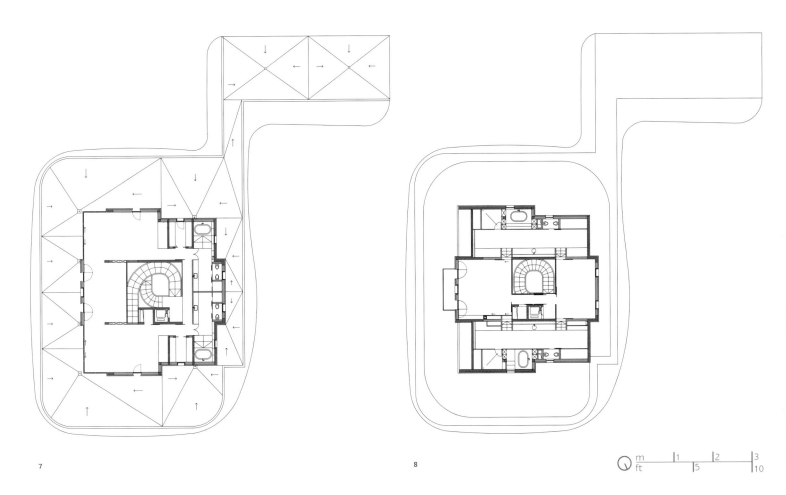

7   8

1

1. The form of a cricket oval inspired the sunken 'pit' in the centre of the upper level extension. A clerestory window floods the space with light.

2. The original double-pitched roof was removed. Timber joists laid across the masonry walls carry the weight of the addition.

Violin House

Melbourne | Australia | Cassandra Complex | Space added: 150m² (1,615ft²)

'I think of it as a house on top of a house,' says Josh Abrahams, Melbourne-based musician and producer. 'The new addition is my home; the original bungalow is now my recording studio.'

Abrahams bought the 1950s bungalow in 1997. It occupies a generous plot in leafy Brighton, one of Melbourne's bay-side suburbs. The building was rendered all but invisible from the street by mature trees and a high front fence, but a dark interior was the payoff for privacy.

Abrahams' decision to extend the property was motivated by a desire to work from home; he also wanted to stop paying rent on a studio. He invited young Melbourne architect Cassandra Fahey, whose practice is called Cassandra Complex, to design a second level.

Fahey rose to prominence in 2001 by designing a private house with a picture of Pamela Anderson emblazoned on the glass façade for a television presenter. She followed this up with the Chameleon, an 'internal' extension in the form of an amorphous sculpture clad in red glass tiles that encloses a staircase, bedroom, study area and bathroom (see introduction, page 17) in her boyfriend's apartment. She has a reputation for flamboyant, attention-grabbing architecture, and she borrows freely from popular culture.

'I gave Josh a number of different options for the extension. They were

2

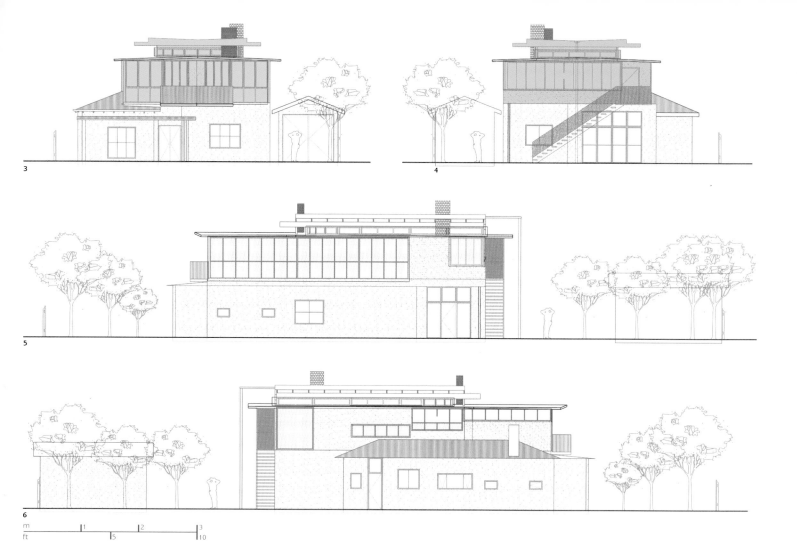

3

4

5

6

m
ft
|1 |2 |3
|5 |10

3 South elevation

4 North elevation

5 West elevation

6 East elevation

7 A Juliet balcony and full height windows lend presence to the previously nondescript street-facing façade.

8 The addition is defined by a palette of dark Jarrah (an Australian hardwood) and coloured tiles.

spontaneous designs. One was the Sunflower House; another was the Cricket Pitch House, which was based around an oval,' says Fahey. He chose the second, albeit with a different spin. 'Josh doesn't like cricket, but he did like the arrangement of the living spaces around a sunken "pit",' explains Fahey, who now refers to the building as the Violin House, a reference to the significance of music and acoustics in the design.

The new level is accessed via an external staircase to the rear of the property. Ascending the thick treads of recycled jarrah – a dark, oily, native Australian hardwood – the visitor walks onto a platform overlooking the sunken dining oval in the centre which doubles as a private performance space. At floor level the form is defined by a skirting of green tiles. A clerestory window defines the roof level and allows natural light to flood in; only sky and treetops are visible, belying the dense residential setting.

A galley kitchen runs along the eastern edge of the oval; a study area with Japanese-style built-in shelves is opposite. At the end of the large open-plan volume is a short passage that offers access to a large bathroom, smaller shower-room and two bedrooms at the front of the house. The two bedrooms both have access to a Juliet balcony that gives presence to the previously nondescript façade.

The extension is clad throughout in dark-stained recycled jarrah. Coloured tiles define different uses: green for the kitchen and bathrooms, orange for the balcony, red for the corner fireplace. Patterned glass along the east façade lends another dimension to the distinctive decorative palette.

9 Floor plan of the first floor: the staircase to the new
level is positioned at the rear of the building.

10 The oval offers access to a large bathroom, shower
room and two bedrooms at the front of the house.

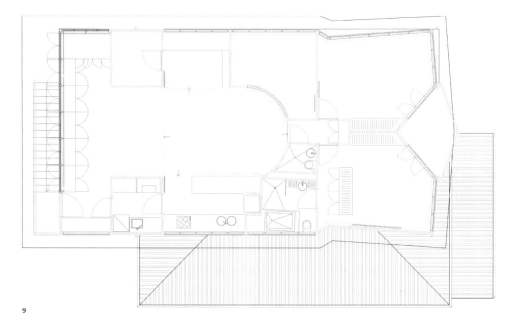

9

The addition of the second level required
the removal of the existing double-pitched
tiled roof. To carry its weight timber joists
were laid across the masonry walls. Only
one steel post was required, to support the
rear entrance overhang.

The work cost approximately A$500,000
($370,000). Design and construction were
completed in 18 months.

1

1 Patrick and Sabah Friedrich's apartment occupies the top floor and roof of a 1960s building in the centre of Merzig. Their hairdressing salon is on the ground floor.

2 The building before the extension was added.

3 Plans of the upper and lower levels. 1) kitchen, 2) dining room, 3) bedroom, 4) bathroom, 5) corridor, 6) living room, 7) winter garden, 8) roof deck, 9) roof garden.

Symbiont Friedrich extension

Merzig | **Germany** | **FloSundK architektur + urbanistik** | **Space added: 40m² (430 ft²)**

2

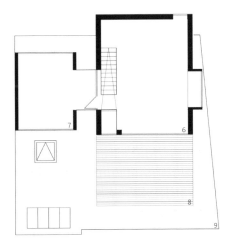

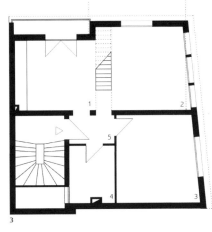

3

m | 1 | 2 | 3
ft | 5 | 10

Patrick Friedrich is a tall man, which is useful in his profession – he and his wife Sabah are hairdressers – but which was a significant drawback in the couple's dark, cramped, low-ceilinged apartment. However, height wasn't the only problem. The Friedrichs were also frustrated by the apartment's limited size, and wanted much more external space than their small north-facing balcony could offer.

So the conundrum facing architects FloSundK, a young practice based in nearby Saarbrücken, was how to increase the size of apartment and create a roof garden with a limited budget on a prominent site in the heart of the town.

The first challenge was to secure planning consent. 'We wanted to make as much use of the roof area as possible. Originally, 30 per cent of the floor area of the two rooftop boxes projected over the side of the building,' explains architect Jens Stahnke. The proposal was rejected, as was a subsequent iteration. The third proposal still extended slightly over the edge, but by that stage the mayor of Merzig, a small town close to the borders with France and Luxembourg, had become embroiled in the debate. He and his wife are regular and satisfied customers at the Friedrich's hairdressing salon, on the ground floor of the building. His influence was critical in convincing the planners to accept the architect's proposal.

There was another challenge to overcome, however, in the form of local disenchantment with the contemporary design. The architects were determined that the rooftop addition be in stark contrast with the original building, an unremarkable structure faced in cream and blue tiles. 'We didn't want to mimic the 1960s style, but design something with its own distinct character,' says Stahnke. On the street-facing south elevation they proposed two boxes: a living space, with walls of dark grey reinforced chipboard, and a 'winter garden' wrapped in untreated zinc. A pre-cast concrete firewall painted a vivid green was put forward for the east elevation.

Construction took about 11 months. Before work began on the roof, the apartment itself was remodelled. The principal alterations were the removal of an internal wall separating the living space and kitchen, and the insertion of a lightweight steel staircase to the rooftop, which also doubles as a light well.

The rooftop itself was divided into three areas: the two lightweight timber-framed boxes, which were prefabricated off-site and craned into place in sections, and the external space, which comprises a decked area surrounded by a planted garden.

While the Friedrichs were delighted with their remodelled and enlarged home, and the scheme was awarded a prestigious BDA Prize (2004), it was not until it was selected to represent Germany at the 2006 Venice Biennale that the denizens of Merzig came around to the multi-coloured parasite on top of the hairdressers. 'They have realized that people actually visit Merzig because they have heard about it. It has become an attraction,' says Stahnke.

4

5

6

7

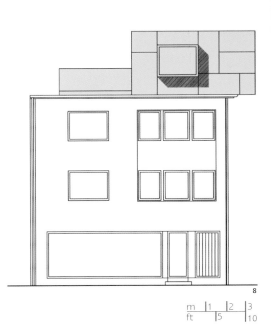

8

m |1 |2 |3
ft |5 |10

chapter 2
Back & front

1

1 The rear extension is composed of two interlocking boxes clad in stained timber rain screen. It encloses a bathroom (first floor), family room (ground floor) and a pre-cast concrete wine cellar.

2 The new two-storey extension has approximately the same volume as the low, long 1970s conservatory that it has replaced.

57 South Hill Park

London | UK | Robert Dye Associates | Space added: ground floor 26m² (280ft²); first floor 18m² (194ft²)

2

Typically, architects win commissions based on recommendations from satisfied customers, or through architecture books like this one. Very rarely does a job materialize from an invitation to house-sit, but that is what happened at 57 South Hill Park, a four-storey Edwardian semi-detached property in a North London conservation area.

At the time, Robert Dye's own home was undergoing renovation, and Elizabeth and Gabriel Irwin, the owners of 57 South Hill Park, invited him to house-sit while they were abroad on holiday. As a parting joke it was suggested that while he was there Dye might take a look at the 'rotten extension and leaky roof . . . and think of a use for the bit of wasted space at the back'. The Irwins were taken at their word.

As well as replacing the awkward 1970s rear extension and plugging the hole in the roof, Dye took on the challenge of making the interior more appropriate to twenty-first-century family life, creating lighter, brighter and larger spaces. Gabriel Irwin's memories of 'inside/outside' Modernism in India were another inspiration: as a child, he had visited a house designed by Le Corbusier which had left a lasting impression.

The original extension was long and low. Its replacement is shorter and two storeys high. Planning consent was granted because the new extension is approximately the same volume as the old one.

3 A large circular skylight allows light to flood into the ground-level family room.

4 Bi-fold doors connect the family room to the decked outdoor eating area; on the inside, slot windows frame views of the garden.

5 The dark timber of the extension is a deliberate counterpoint to the pale brickwork of the original house.

Externally the two dark timber-clad interlocking cubes are a deliberate counterpoint to the pale original brickwork. Internally the sequence of spaces blends harmoniously with the original house.

At ground-floor level, the extension contains a large family room between the kitchen and the garden. South-facing bi-fold doors open onto the garden, creating a seamless segue to the newly decked outdoor eating area.

The upper cube holds a substantial bathroom, whose sandblasted glass end-screen lets light in while ensuring privacy. Smaller side-windows frame views of the London skyline.

Dye also undertook the renovation of the top floor in the existing house, adding two new bedrooms and a bathroom. On the floor below, a rearrangement of the internal partitions and the installation of a new shower-room created approximately 20 per cent more usable space.

From its unconventional origins, Dye's work on 57 South Hill Park evolved into a comprehensive and highly effective overhaul, giving a cramped, dark Edwardian house a new lease of life.

The design and completion of the work took almost three years at a cost of over £300,000 ($550,000).

3

4

5

6 Cross-section looking north: 1) Bedroom, 2) Bathroom, 3) Bedroom, 4) Bedroom, 5) Sitting-room, 6) Master bedroom, 7) Kitchen, 8) Dining-room, 9) Family room, 10) Wine cellar

7 Sandblasted glass filters light in the new bathroom; smaller side windows frame views of London's skyline.

8 The dining area links the kitchen to the new family room at the rear.

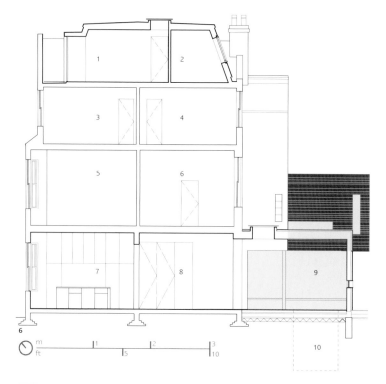

6

It was suggested that Dye might take a look at the 'rotten extension and leaky roof . . . and think of a use for the bit of wasted space at the back'

7

1

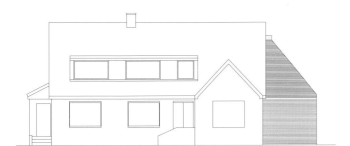

2

Bell-Simpson House

Stirlingshire │ UK │ NORD Architecture │ Space added: 115m² (1,238ft²)

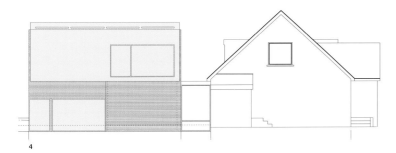

3

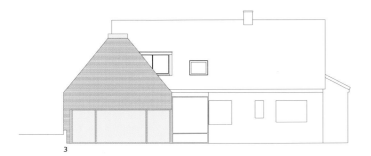

4

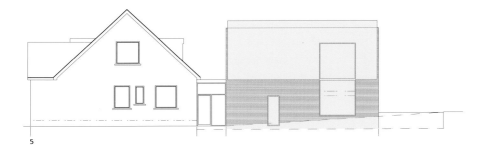

5

All over the world, farmers add outhouses as demand dictates. The tradition in rural Stirlingshire, a landlocked county in the heart of Scotland, is no different.

Typically, outhouses were attached to or within easy reach of the main house, to allow access to livestock; they might also double as a windbreak. In every case the outcome was based on a logic born of necessity. The same could be said of the extension to the Bell-Simpson house, a 1950s dormer bungalow with uninterrupted views of the Campsie Hills.

The clients wanted two new living spaces and a study, but there was no room within the existing storey-and-a-half-high house. An outhouse was the only option.

Technically, to conform to local planning guidelines, an extension should blend seamlessly with the existing house. In this case, the architects – a young Glasgow practice, NORD Architecture – managed to build a convincing case for the honesty and rationality of their design outcome based on local traditions of agricultural development.

It is only superficially that the extension deviates from the planning guidelines; its form and dimensions are derived entirely from the original building. In place of darker bricks and tiles, the architects used red bricks and clay tiles, creating a sympathetic but demonstrably distinct structure.

As well as replicating the uniformity of the original building, the envelope of the

6 A full-length rooflight set along the ridge of the roof allows light to flood the open-plan upper level.

7 The transition between the original house and the extension is marked by a flat-roofed glass corridor, which is also used as a new entrance to the house.

8 Ground-level floor plan

9 Upper-level floor plan

extension was stripped of articulation and expression. All components – roof, walls, windows and doors – are pulled flush to the outer face of the structure, so there is no hierarchy between elements.

The extension is positioned behind the original building. As the landscape rises to the north, the building form is stepped down into the landscape. A retaining wall wraps around three sides of the extension, reinforcing the sense of protection and enclosure.

Internally there is a clear contrast between the two storeys. At ground level the ceiling has been kept deliberately low, at 2.25 metres (7 feet 5 inches), and extensive use has been made of glazing – full-height sliding doors open onto the small enclosed courtyard. On the upper level, the roof reaches a full storey and a half; the space feels light and airy.

The focal point of the upper level is a full-length rooflight set along the ridge and raised on powder-coated-aluminium upstands. On the east-facing façade a technically innovative folded window wraps from the roof to the hip of the extension and down to the lower level.

A single-storey glazed flat-roofed box marks the transition point between the original dormer bungalow and the brick-clad extension. It doubles as an additional point of entry to the house proper.

6

7

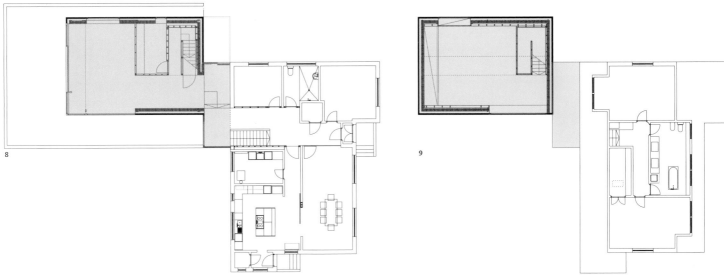

8

9

1

1 The roof of the rear extension tilts up, to attract winter sun and limit the glare of strong summer rays; dark tiles retain heat and enhance the room's solar performance.

2 Frank Caristo's 1930s bungalow is heritage-protected, meaning that its front façade has not been altered.

3 A view of the rear lean-to before work began.

Caristo House

Sydney | Australia | Sam Crawford Architects | Space added: 55m² (592ft²)

In the 1930s, when Frank Caristo's bungalow was built, Australians still lived like the British. Homes were small, dark brick-built affairs that made few concessions to the local climate.

It wasn't until the 1950s, with the influx of Mediterranean Europeans displaced by World War II, that things began to change. Only then did Australians begin to develop forms of residential architecture appropriate to their own climate and social conventions.

The Caristo House, in the Sydney suburb of Croydon, provides vivid evidence of this evolution. Its boxy, red brick front façade is protected from the road by a small patch of grass, reminiscent of a street in Croydon's British namesake. In stark contrast its rear extension actively attracts natural light, and breaks down the barrier between external and interior spaces.

Frank Caristo is a design-savvy hydraulic engineer descended from Italian stock. In 2003 he and his wife began to consider ways of overhauling the rear of their bungalow. The first stage involved the preparation a brief, which included the replacement of existing 1960s lean-to with a new living area, kitchen, laundry and bathroom. An external seating area and barbeque were other requirements. Caristo was prepared to sacrifice some of the back garden, but not all of it - at the time of writing, there were no children, but that may not always be the case.

2

3

4 The open-plan kitchen and dining area opens onto
  the garden with its new built-in barbecue facilities.

5 Cross-section looking north-west, showing the
  original pitched-roof house (on the right of the
  drawing), and the north-facing extension with gently
  ascending roofline (left).

6 The dark, heavy rooms at the front of the house are a
  stark contrast with the white and airy rear extension.

Stage two involved inviting three architects to draw up plans in response to the brief; the Caristos made their selections from architecture and interior magazines. Each received a small fee.

The successful architect was Sam Crawford, one of Sydney's up-and-coming young architects who has made his name designing houses for well-heeled locals. 'Frank was a great client. He knew what he wanted, he knew what architects do and he respected our advice,' says Crawford. Unusually, Caristo also took on the challenge of building the extension.

The body of the volume comprises a large open-plan kitchen and dining and seating area, which opens on to the north-facing garden. The space is overwhelmingly white, to attract light through the full-width sliding/folding doors.

Dark tiles pave the floor, to retain heat and enhance the room's solar performance. The tiled area extends beyond the doors into the garden itself, reinforcing the links between the external and internal areas, and creating an unbroken link between the extension and the covered seating area in the garden itself.

The roof of the extension has been tilted upwards by 30 degrees, the optimum angle to catch the winter sun while blocking the oppressively hot summer rays. A row of glazed louvers above the sliding/folding doors allows air to circulate at night, and partially screens the unlovely views of Sydney's western suburbs. The side walls of the extension screen views of neighbouring properties, and help to enclose the garden.

The extension and adjacent garage are built around cold-form sheet frames, a system often used in factory buildings.

4

In the 1950s Australians began to develop forms of residential architecture appropriate to their own climate and social conventions

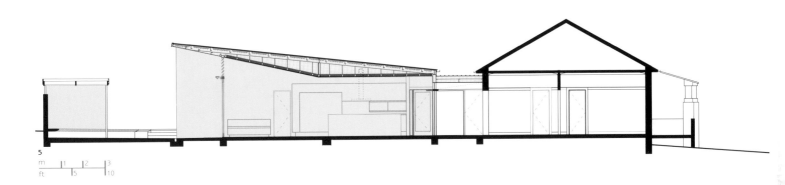

5

m | |1 | |2 | |3
ft | |5 | |10

6

7 Full-width sliding/folding doors dissolve the barrier
between external and internal areas; the glazed
louvres above allow air to circulate at night.

'It was a way of saving time during construction,' says Crawford. The industrial theme is continued in the box section steel roofing panels.

There was one hitch during an otherwise seamless design and construction process. The Caristo's house is one of a group of five heritage-protected bungalows, which meant that any alterations required the consent of the local authority. Unfortunately the view of Burwood Council's heritage consultant did not coincide with the shared view of Caristo and Crawford. 'We felt strongly that the best way to respect the heritage listed building was to build an extension that was overtly new, not to design a poor imitation of the past,' says Crawford. The wrangle caused delays and friction, but did not ultimately make impact on the quality or effectiveness of the finished product.

The work took 12 months to complete at a cost of A$300,000 (£125,000).

1

1 To maximize light gain and increase the previously restricted height of the ceiling, the extension slopes from north to south.

2 The brief was to replace the original rear lean-to, turn the garden into an outdoor room and overhaul the front end of the house.

3 Polychromatic bi-directional steel panels mark out the extension as a new addition and create a feature in the cobbled lane to the north.

Clifton Hill rear extension

Melbourne | Australia | Adam Dettrick | Space added: 39m² (420ft²)

Planning ahead can help to avoid knee-jerk, quick-fix solutions to space-creating quandaries. Nobody benefits from a dark and depressing basement or an ill-considered loft. Designing an effective extension takes time, and anticipating changes in lifestyle is a part of the process.

The owners of this two-storey late-nineteenth-century terrace house in Clifton Hill, one of Melbourne's suburbs, actually live in the Victorian Outback, but they plan to retire to Melbourne. In preparation they asked architect Adam Dettrick to renovate and extend their city home.

The brief was threefold: to replace the rear kitchen lean-to, turn the garden into an outdoor room with space for off-street parking, and spruce up the tired front end of the house, with an emphasis on improved circulation and the projection of natural light into the dark interior.

In its original format, the lean-to ran along the southern boundary of the back garden. To maximize light gain and increase the previously restricted ceiling height, Dettrick decided to twist the new extension by 90 degrees. This involved knocking down a section of the rear wall and constructing a timber-framed single-storey addition to the full width of the house.

Mimicking the profile of the original lean-to, the roof of the extension has been designed at a gentle incline; it reaches up to the northern sun, and slopes down to the

3

4 The kitchen/dining-room acts as the link between the living-room and the new back garden.

5 North elevation: corrugated-metal roller doors (on the right) open onto the rear garden, which doubles as an off-street parking space.

6 Rear elevation

7 Floor plan

8 A deep reveal acts as a shield from the elements; the floor is made of bricks recycled from the partially demolished original rear façade.

top of the southern partition wall, avoiding any impact on the neighbours' sight-lines.

Light floods the interior through a long deep-set window that runs along the top of the north-facing façade and abuts another window running top to bottom at the house-end, creating an inverted 'L'.

The new northern façade makes a bold statement in the cobbled lane that runs alongside the house. Dettrick used polychromatic bi-directional steel panels to create a decorative effect that both marks out the addition as demonstrably new and blends with the gracefully rusting corrugated-iron fences and roofs that are such a feature of Australia's landscapes.

Internally, the extension offers a completely different spatial arrangement from that of the original building. The kitchen occupies the southern wall; the laundry has been reduced in size and hidden within the kitchen cupboards. Dettrick has capitalized on this rearrangement by enhancing the connections between the extension and the existing parts of the house. The most significant alteration was the partial removal of the living-room wall, opening it up to the extension.

Flooring materials define the sequence of internal and external spaces, from carpet in the old part of the house through to limestone slabs in the extension and recycled bricks in the back garden. The thermal mass of the stone floor has been used to augment that of the existing masonry building and to offset the heat-flows associated with the glazing in the dining area.

The total cost of the renovation and expansion was A$190,000 ($139,000), of which approximately 50 per cent was spent on the extension itself.

7

m |1 |2 |3
ft |10

8

1

1 A 15-metre (50-foot) *Podocarpus* tree with sentimental value to the Lee family has been brought within the boundaries of the house.

2 Torrey Lee bought the original white-walled bungalow from his aunt. The building has been in the family for three generations.

3 A steel-framed timber screen 5.5 metres (18 feet) from the side walls encloses the house and creates 'outdoor rooms' which make the most of the Californian climate.

Lee Residence

La Jolla | California | USA | Public | Space added: 325m² (3,500ft²)

A wrap-around timber screen and new second storey have rendered the Lee family's residence all but unrecognizable as the small white stucco bungalow that they enclose. But despite the upheaval one feature has remained constant: the mature *Podocarpus* tree in the front yard.

The tree, a tall evergreen only three feet from the south-west corner of the original house, has sentimental significance for Torrey Lee. It was there when his grandmother bought the simple ranch house in 1949 where his mother was brought up, and Lee remembers swinging from a rope slung over one of its branches during childhood visits. So when his grandmother died and the opportunity arose to buy the house from his aunt, Lee and his wife could not resist. In 2003 they relocated from their large loft apartment in downtown San Diego to the small Californian beach community of La Jolla, a 25-minute drive away.

From the outset it was clear that more space would be required. The Lees have two young daughters; the bungalow contained only two bedrooms and one bathroom. It was also very dark, but despite the tree's proximity to the house, Lee was adamant that it must stay.

A number of architects were approached for advice, including San Diego practice Public, a recommendation of Lee's sister. Public partners James Gates and Jim Brown

2

3

4 The physical footprint of the bungalow has not expanded. Space was added on top of and around the building.

5 The tree plays a functional role, shading the house from the strong sun.

6 The spacing of the timber slats varies depending on the requirement for privacy. At the front the screen is almost solid, concealing the garage and an entrance to the front deck.

were the only architects who expressed any enthusiasm for retaining the tree. They were appointed as both architect and general contractor; in the USA, a contractor supplies all labour, materials and project management.

The first stage in the transformation of the bungalow into a three-bedroom, two-bathroom family house was to consult a tree specialist, who advised Gates and Brown on ways to minimize damage to the tree's extensive root-system. They then stripped the house back to its bare bones.

To avoid a full coastal review process, 50 per cent of the existing exterior stud-walls had to be left standing, and the building footprint could not be expanded. The solution to this zoning constraint was to surround the house with a steel-framed screen filled in with timber slats, creating 'outdoor rooms' at the front and rear and along the sides to increase the liveable area of the house without contravening regulations. The screen, which allows in the temperate sea breezes while controlling the late-afternoon sun, also encloses the *Podocarpus*, bringing it within the bosom of the family and harnessing its foliage for sun-shading.

On the interior, the once cramped ground-floor living space has been transformed into a double-height kitchen and dining area, with access to the outdoor rooms at the front and rear. The small front windows have become full-height sliding doors that let light flood in and allow access to the enclosed front deck.

The second-storey addition incorporates the children's two bedrooms, each of which has a balcony, a bathroom and a study.

4

7 The second storey has been cut away to create a double-height family space, dining-room and kitchen.

8 Storage is built into the staircase, maximizing the available space.

8

To conform to planning regulations, 50 per cent of the existing exterior stud-walls were left standing and the building's footprint was not expanded

1

2

1 The extension triples the size of the house and establishes a strong relationship with the long front garden.

2 The original house, hemmed in at the end of the narrow plot, was subject to strict constraints concerning increases to the liveable floor area.

3 A winding path through the centre of the garden leads to the new front entrance.

Patio House

Nantes | France | Michelle Pasquier | Space added: approximately 80m² (860ft²)

This extension to a small single-façade dwelling hemmed in at the end of a long narrow site was subject to strict constraints. The plot ratio allowed only a slight increase in liveable floor area. But the client's young family was in urgent need of space. 'What was needed was a ploy to create an impression of added space over and above reality,' says architect Michelle Pasquier.

Other requirements of the brief were to bring daylight into the interior of the house, and to keep within a tight budget – €1,000 per square metre ($119 per square foot). The outcome effectively triples the size of the house.

The design hinges around a 16-square-metre (172-square-foot) square patio in the centre of the extension. It is open to the elements, which means that it does not count as floor space, but the reality of day-to-day domestic life means that it has found a number of functions: as a safe place for the children to play in, as an open-air living-room and as a tranquil, green oasis in the heart of the home.

On the side adjacent to the original house, the patio is bordered by the kitchen, bathroom and toilets. On the eastern edge, a spacious living and dining area with full-height sliding doors creates a seamless transition into the long garden. A teak deck further extends the living-room. The bedrooms are located in the remodelled original section of the house.

4 The 16-square-metre (172-square-foot) patio in the centre of the extension is open to the elements, which means that it does not count as floor space in the eyes of the planners.

5 Axonometric view showing the open-air patio in the centre of the extension.

6 Cross-section showing the new front extension next to the original structure.

7 The patio is flanked by a kitchen (pictured right), and bathroom, toilet and utility rooms (left); the front section functions as a multi-purpose family space.

As well as responding to the brief and conforming to planning regulations, the patio completely opens up the house, in the process creating unexpected sight-lines and marking a clear distinction between the living and service areas. It also defines circulation patterns and spatial arrangements.

The choice of materials reflects both the budget and the ingenuity of the design approach. The walls of the timber-framed extension are composed of plaster block walls, concrete posts support the structure, and the roof is covered in zinc sheeting.

The total cost of the project was €144,000 ($185,000). It was completed within 12 months.

4

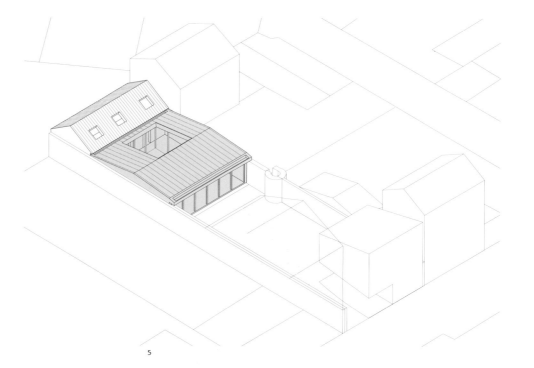

5

The plot ratio allowed only a slight increase in liveable floor area.
But the client's young family was in urgent need of space

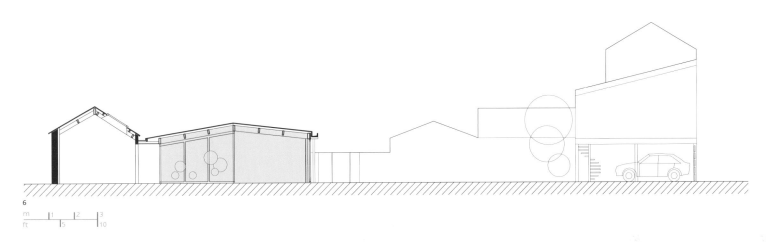

6

8 The patio creates unexpected sight-lines and opens up the house; it also marks the distinction between the living and service areas.

9 Open to the elements, the patio functions as a green oasis and a safe place for the children.

10 Site plan: 1) Living-room, 2) Utility space, 3) Bathroom and toilet, 4) Kitchen, 5) Bedrooms, 6) Enclosed courtyard, 7) External deck, 8) Front garden, 9) Garage

9

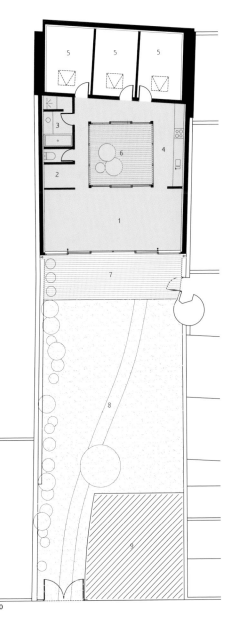

10

1

2

1 The original rear kitchen extension was dark and had no windows looking over the semi-redundant south-facing garden.

2 Sliding/folding doors open the new, light-filled, rear family room to the decked garden.

3 The large rooflight was designed to make a spectacle of the natural environment: the walls act as a canvas for the shifting light and the changeable British weather.

Rear family room

London | UK | Map Projects Ltd | Space added: 20m² (215ft²)

3

Matthew Hutchings and Jasmeen Zafar originally employed architect Pasquale Amodio of Map Projects Ltd to extend and refurbish their kitchen. Two years later, Amodio and his team had completely rearranged the ground floor of the three-storey Victorian house, added a light-filled living space at the back and made the garden a functional feature of the house for the first time in its 150-year history. The cost of the work was £65,000 ($120,000).

The original rear lean-to comprised a dining area, a kitchen and a toilet accessible from the exterior. The single-storey structure was dark, and had no windows looking over the semi-redundant garden. 'It was Pasquale who encouraged us to consider using the space as a living-room. It has worked brilliantly,' says Zafar.

Preliminary investigations revealed that the structural integrity of the lean-to would be compromised by the removal of its internal walls. Amodio suggested that it be demolished in its entirety, and proposed a new volume that was higher and would extend into the garden. In principle the idea sounded good, but Amodio's proposal would also require the reconfiguration of all the rooms on the ground floor. Fortunately his clients were open to the idea.

Like many terraced houses of its vintage, the property was designed with a living-room overlooking the street, a drawing-room in the middle of the space,

4 Floor plan

5 Over a period of two years the house was completely rearranged. In the process, the garden became a functional feature of the ground floor for the first time in 150 years.

and a dining/kitchen area at the back. 'We proposed that the kitchen be positioned in the middle of the ground floor and that the dining-room overlook the street, similar to houses in Holland,' says Amodio. This left the south-facing rear void free for use as a secluded and light-filled living area.

The rear extension was designed to make a spectacle of the weather. Its white walls act as a canvas for the constantly shifting light patterns and the vagaries of the British climate. Natural light floods the space: the roof is a single pane of glass; folding doors open onto the decked garden.

Since completion, the top-lit timber-clad box has become the room in which Hutchings, Zafar and their two young children spend most of their time. It accommodates a sofa, a television, audio equipment, bookshelves and play-space.

'Although it has slightly reduced the size of the garden, we've found that we actually make much more use of the outdoor space,' says Zafar. 'It really brings the outside in. Even during the winter, when the folding door is often shut, we are so much more aware of nature and the changing seasons.'

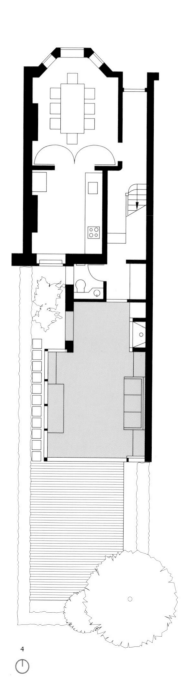

4

1 The house is framed and protected by a canopy of 89 solar panels, one of several devices used by architect owners Angela Brooks and Lawrence Scarpa to optimize opportunities for sustainable living.

2 The original Spanish-style bungalow was built on a narrow through-plot in the 1920s.

3 As part of the overhaul the original north-facing entrance has become the rear of the property.

Solar Umbrella House

Venice | California | USA | Pugh + Scarpa | Space added: 116m² (1,250ft²)

Sustainable, low-emission architecture is not exclusive to new builds. A carefully considered extension can help a home rise above the apparent limitations of the original structure.

In 1997, architect couple Angela Brooks and Lawrence Scarpa – both principals of Santa Monica practice Pugh + Scarpa – bought a small Spanish-style bungalow (c.1923) on a long narrow plot running roughly north-south in a residential district of Venice, California.

They made some minimal alterations but essentially left the house untouched for the first five years: plenty of time to become attuned to the cycle of the seasons and local environmental conditions. It was 2002 before they started work on the extension.

To make a virtue of the searing Californian sun, the house has been extended towards the south. This involved realigning it by 180 degrees – the original Boccaccio Avenue entrance is now the rear – and designing a new frontage to face Woodlawn Avenue.

The new south-facing façade is framed by a canopy of 89 solar panels which protect the body of the building from thermal heat gain. The solar skin also transforms the heat into usable energy, providing 100 per cent of the residence's electricity. The payback period for the panels is about seven years.

The original bungalow has been left almost completely untouched. The kitchen,

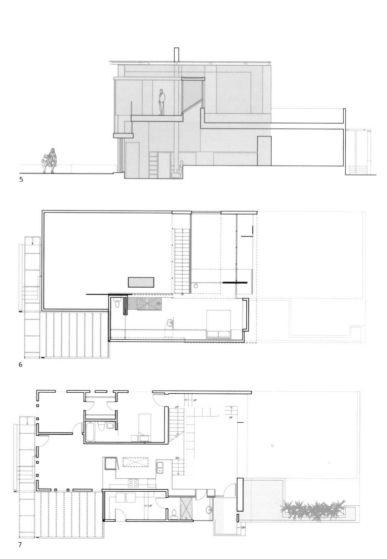

4

5

6

7

4 Passive and solar design strategies mean that the house is 100 per cent energy neutral.

5 Cross-section looking west

6 Upper-level floor plan

7 Ground-floor plan

8 The first-floor terrace is shaded by the solar canopy; the master bedroom runs along the western side of the upper level.

dining-room, bathroom and two lower-level bedrooms remain in their original positions. Only the south wall was removed, to accommodate the new two-storey steel-framed extension, which contains a high-ceilinged living space, a master bedroom, a utility room, storage and an entrance. Extensive use of glass means that there are now unbroken sight-lines through the house.

A staircase of folded plate steel that appears to float in space offers access to the new bedroom and open-air terrace. The illusion of weightlessness is a theme carried throughout the extension: the delicate interaction of voids and solids with the natural environment creates the impression that the building touches the ground extremely lightly.

Recycled materials and environmentally responsive features have been used throughout the house, many integrated as design elements. The solar panels are only the most explicit.

Typically, solar panels are hidden away on the roof, but in this particular example Brooks and Scarpa have used them to define the building envelope and provide shelter. On the interior, the bespoke cabinets in the living space have been finished with fibreboard made from recycled newspaper (Homasote); the principal flooring material is compressed woodchips bound with high-strength adhesive, a cost-effective and morally preferable alternative to hardwoods.

Dedication to responsible twenty-first-century living also extends to the external areas. All rainwater is retained on site and diverted to plants via a dry well underneath the garden.

8

9 Homasote (pulped newspaper) was used to finish the cabinets in the new living space; the floor is made of compressed woodchips bound with high-strength adhesive.

10 The staircase of folded plate steel appears to float in space.

11 All furniture and fittings were designed by Brooks and Scarpa.

Scarpa and Brooks' home was inspired by Paul Rudolph's Umbrella House, a Modernist structure built in 1953 in Sarasota, Florida and named after the overhanging wooden trellis that shaded it from the elements. In 2005 it became only the third building ever to be auctioned as a work of art; bids started at $1.2 million. Philip Johnson's Rockefeller Guest House and the Farnsworth House designed by Mies van der Rohe were the first.

The Solar Umbrella House is unlikely to follow suit. It is stylish and abstract, but it is not a work of art. Rather it is a highly commendable landmark of cost-effective, place-specific, self-sufficient residential architecture.

9

The original
bungalow has
been left almost
untouched.
Only the south wall
was removed, to
accommodate the
two-storey steel-
framed extension

10

11

1 The annexe extends into the rear of the original house, which required extensive alterations to the arrangement of the ground floor.

2 The rear extension rests on two pre-existing parallel foundation walls. Construction involved pouring 75 tonnes of concrete into the formwork that extends deep into the house.

The weight of an extension is rarely the determining factor in its composition or form. Of course, structural requirements may demand the selection of lightweight materials for a rooftop addition, but in typical circumstances colour, height or style is much more likely to influence what an extension actually looks like. That was not the case with this ground-level rear extension and renovation to a 1970s property in Pittsford, New York.

The clients, two doctors in their fifties, wanted a substantial addition to their home. They invited Iran-born, US-educated architect Mehrdad Hadighi to put forward some proposals. 'The first actually shrank the house, by removing all of the small protrusions from the back and the roof, and returning it to a simple T-shape plan,' says Hadighi. 'The other essentially kept the same area, but altered the space of the interior and the enclosed porch.' His clients opted for the second.

For Hadighi, an architect noted for experimentation, the commission became an opportunity to explore the relationship between the existing 185-square-metre (1,990-square-foot) white vinyl-siding-clad house and a rear extension made of polished black concrete. The first appears temporary; the second implies permanence. Each weighs 75 tonnes.

1

Tall Acres

Pittsford | **New York** | **USA** | **Studio for Architecture** | **Space added: rear extension 44m² (474ft²); bathroom 7.5m² (81 ft²)**

3 To achieve the smoothest possible finish, the black-pigmented concrete was formed in acrylic-faced plywood and then hand-polished to a shine and sealed.

4 The large rear extension includes the kitchen and dining area.

The concrete addition rests on two existing parallel foundation walls, and cantilevers into and out of the house, counterbalancing its weight, colour and structure. It is based, according to Hadighi, on an oppositional matrix. On a more prosaic level, the avoidance of excavation and foundation work helped to minimize expenditure; the work cost $148,000.

Because the extension actually projects into the house, substantial remodelling work was also carried out on the interior. The architects removed all the false ceilings to give a more 'cathedral-like' quality, and transformed a guest bedroom into a bridge that spans the living space.

Dr Mohammad Salahuddin and Anwara Begum use the extension for their kitchen and dining area; the original parts of the house comprise the living spaces and bedrooms. In 2005 they invited Hadighi back to discuss the addition of a bathroom.

The bathroom continues the experiment with opposites: in this case it is in opposition to the concrete monolith, not to the original house. The use of a colourful, fragile and light material is the intentional antithesis of the heavy, indestructible black concrete. It was also designed to bring light into the dark heart of the house. 'It is much like a lantern to the interior during the day, and to the exterior at night,' says Hadighi.

In 2003, Hadighi was selected by *Architectural Record* as one of the world's ten most promising young architects. He was cited for the 'disciplined ordering of materials, to make theory visible'. His work at Tall Acres is a good example of this 'theory made action' side of his work.

3

4

The polished black concrete counterbalances
the weight, colour and form of the white
house. The delicate bathroom of green glass
contrasts with the concrete

5

6

5 The green-glazed bathroom introduces a source of light into the dark heart of the house.

6 The bathroom protrudes above the roof of the original house. At night it resembles a glowing lantern.

7 Diagram looking south

8 First-floor plan with the new bathroom in the centre.

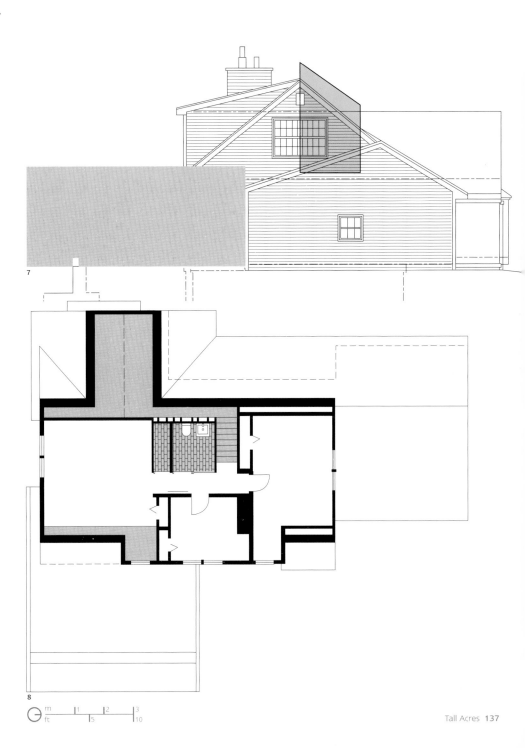

chapter 3

Sideways

1

1 The rear façade of the side extension is almost entirely glazed, to let light into the interior, and to connect the house to the garden – landscaped by Jinny Blom.

2 The plot was previously used as a double garage.

3 Three distinct elements have been used to articulate the street-facing façade: a thin 'slot' of opaque frameless glass links the starkly contemporary birch-clad extension and the existing Victorian frontage.

50 Pilgrim's Lane

London | UK | Eldridge Smerin | Space added: 185m² (1,990ft²)

When rare-book dealer Bernard Shapero and his wife Emma bought a derelict Victorian house in Hampstead, London, they were not planning to commission an award-winning work of contemporary architecture – but that is what they got.

As well as stripping out and remodelling the interior of the existing house, architects Nick Eldridge and Piers Smerin – who had been recommended to the Shaperos by friends – proposed an extension onto an adjacent site previously occupied by a double garage, effectively doubling the size of the house.

Far from designing an imitation of the redbrick nineteenth-century original, the architects envisioned the extension as starkly contemporary. The Shaperos, already supporters of the architects' simple, understated style, approved the idea. 'We didn't want to build a reproduction Victorian home, so it made sense to go for something modern and new,' they say.

The mute façade of the new steel-framed cube has been clad with sheets of birch plywood. Its surface is broken only by a 'slot' of frameless glass that allows light into the kitchen, and a screened area on the second floor, which on warm days becomes an enclosed balcony – it has a glass roof and sliding/folding doors.

To mark the distinction between the new and old elements, Eldridge and Smerin left a full-height gap between them, clad in

4 The three-storey side extension almost doubles the size of the house.

5 Architects Nick Eldridge and Piers Smerin designed the principal fixtures and fittings, including a sideboard unit in the dining-room with a cutlery drawer running the length of the room.

6 The 'slot' of opaque glazing visible on the front façade projects light onto the structural glass staircase, a contrast to the dark, cramped interiors of the original Victorian property.

7 Street-facing elevation

opaque glass panels. As well as letting light into the heart of the integrated property, it encloses the new staircase, which is also composed of structural glass. The height of the extension was established by an existing narrow service wing, which was removed.

Natural light became one of the extension's defining features – the rear façade, overlooking the garden, is entirely glazed.

Another feature is flexibility. Folding doors and sliding screens have been used throughout, creating the potential for the building to be a grand sequence of open-plan volumes or a network of private spaces, depending on need. It is all a long way from the cramped, dark and rigid Victorian original.

The basement in the extension includes a utility room and a large play-space for the Shaperos' three young children. It also offers access to a terrace and the rear garden – designed by Jinny Blom Landscape Design to work harmoniously with the house. The ground floor contains another terrace and the main communal spaces, which have been integrated across both parts of the building to create a seamless blend between the two structures. Four bedrooms are spread across the upper levels.

A focal point is Bernard Shapero's small library, which is enclosed by tiered raked shelving for books, and a glass-topped console unit for manuscripts. The library area forms a balcony overlooking a void carved from the front bay of the existing house which now contains a spiral staircase to the lower level.

The extension and the remodelled original have been finished to an extremely high standard, as might be expected with

5

6

7

8

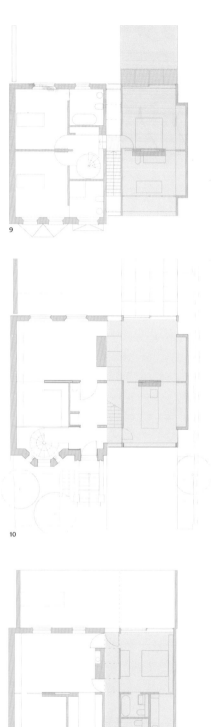

9

10

11

an £850,000 ($1,600,000) budget. But the degree of integration and harmony between all parts of the building, external and internal, is unusually refined.

Part of the reason for this may be that Eldridge and Smerin were responsible for the design of the principal fixtures and fittings, including a reconfigurable series of storage units for the children's bedrooms, and a sideboard unit in the dining-room with a cutlery drawer running the length of the room.

As well as stripping out and remodelling the interior of the existing house, the architects proposed an extension onto an adjacent site

12

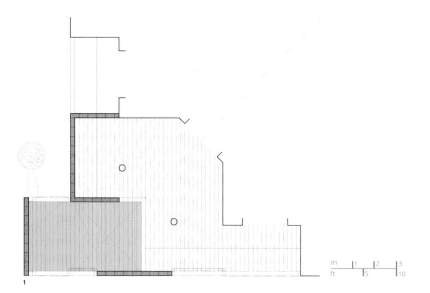

1

2

1 Floor plan

2 The original house was blighted by a small studio and poor connections between the various parts of the building.

3 A double-height tower composed of concrete and polycarbonate sheeting has transformed the character of de los Santos' simple rural home.

Extensions come in all shapes and sizes; they are as varied and idiosyncratic as the people who commission them. Each one is a test of an architect's skill and ingenuity.

The challenge facing Barcelona-based architect Josep Llobet was how to design an artist's studio within an existing rural dwelling in a way that would enhance the building's overall circulation and suitability for its purpose. A small budget added another layer of complexity: the work cost only €19,333 ($24,300).

Since 1989 Jorge de los Santos, an artist who specializes in plastics, has lived in a beautiful woodland setting near the small town of Vidreres, 60 kilometres (37 miles) north of Barcelona.

His broadly triangular home occupies a 100-square-metre (1,076-square-foot) concrete base. Prior to the construction of the new studio it consisted of a sequence of interconnected single-storey volumes with steep tiled roofs. The problem was that his studio was restrictively small. There were also poor connections between the various parts of the building.

Llobet's solution was to remove the building's existing southern corner and replace it with a new tower 5.8 metres (19 feet) high. He also designed an adjacent single-storey workspace with floor-to-ceiling sliding doors, to create an integrated south-eastern façade running flush with the side of the concrete base.

Artist's studio

Vidreres | Spain | Josep Llobet | Space added: 34m² (365ft²)

4 Sun heats the rectangular tower from dawn to dusk.

5 Non-traditional materials were selected for their durability and low cost.

4

The body of the double-height rectangular studio is composed of concrete breeze-blocks and clad with polycarbonate sheeting supported on a lightweight timber frame which separates the concrete blocks from the sheeting by 6 centimetres (2.4 inches). Llobet describes it as a 'ventilated façade system'. Skylights flood the space with natural light.

From the outside it appears to be suspended above the building, an effect accentuated by the lower-level façade of unpolished pine slats and sliding doors set in timber frames. Inside, the connections between the two adjoining spaces have been left exposed, to avoid the use of partitions.

The studio extension may have been cheap and relatively simple to construct, but its scale and the materials used have completely transformed the character of the house.

5

6

6 The remodelling of the house included a single-storey workspace, adjacent to the studio, creating an homogenous south-eastern façade.

7 Sliding doors allow air to circulate.

7

The extension appears to be suspended above the building, an effect accentuated by the lower level façade of unpolished pine slats and sliding doors

1

1 A full-length skylight and rusted metal sculpture punctuate the terrace on top of the underground swimming pool.

2 The cube-shaped extension is a neutral counterpoint to the comparatively decorative existing house.

Casa A-F

Vallvidrera | Spain | exe.arquitectura | Space added: 242m² (2,600ft²)

The clients for this project knew what they wanted – a gym, sauna and swimming pool – but they were not sure how to integrate them without compromising the composition of their early-twentieth-century two-storey family home in Barcelona's Vallvidrera district.

One early plan was to place the new elements and subsidiary spaces – changing rooms, dressing-rooms and external seating areas – within and around the original house, and to place the family's main communal living spaces inside a new side extension.

The architect considered the idea, but it was clear that an above-ground addition would block sight-lines from the main house – Vallvidrera is located in the wooded Collserola hills, 350 metres (1,100 feet) above sea-level, with spectacular views of the city.

The solution was to build part of the extension underground, and to place all the new elements into the annexe, thereby minimizing the disruption to the existing house.

The subterranean swimming pool runs east to west, thus harnessing the natural slope of the site to allow light in at the western end. Only part of the pool is under the annexe, which is accessed via a spiral staircase from the ground-level gym and sauna. The top storey includes a large bathroom and changing area.

3

3 When shut, sliding timber panels enclose the generous terrace and upper-level balconies. When open, they break down the scale of the monolithic cuboid extension.

4 The top storey includes a bathroom and space for changing. A gym and sauna are accommodated on the ground floor.

The extension's rich timber cladding blends discreetly with the earth-coloured tones of the stucco on the original house. The different materials also express the distinction between the new and old elements.

In form, the extension is a stylistically neutral cube, an unornamented counterpoint to the comparatively decorative original house. Sliding doors manipulate the volume; when open, they break down its monolithic form. They also offer access to the garden and balconies.

Ipe, a dark-hued hardwood, was used for the sliding doors and to clad the annexe, as well as for part of the decked area over the swimming pool. Rusted metal sculptures help to break up the surface of the pool covering. An opaque glass skylight runs its full length, reflecting and refracting light in a rainbow of unexpected colours into the pool below.

4

5

5 The subterranean swimming pool cuts into the sloping site, allowing natural daylight in at the western end.

6 Cross-section looking east

7 Plan of the partially submerged swimming pool

8 Cross-section looking south

They were not sure how to integrate the new elements without compromising the composition of their two-storey family home

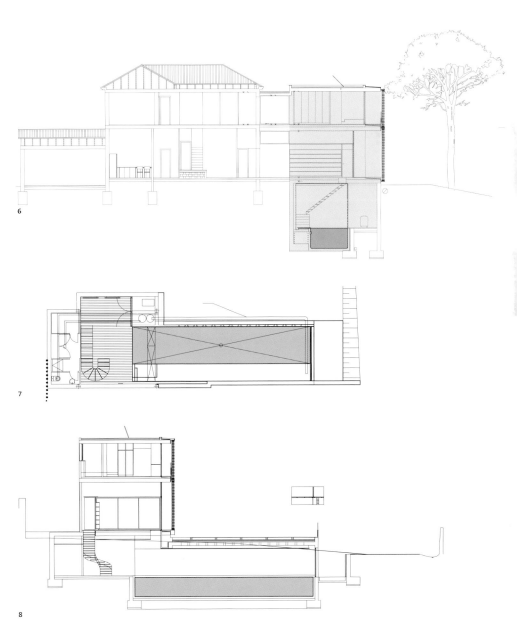

6

7

8

1

1 A new pergola provides shade and creates a linear connection between the white-walled house and the new annexe.

CG Annexe

Caldetas | Spain | Francesc Rifé SL | Space added: 53m² (570ft²)

Caldetas is a quiet and genteel spa town overlooking the Mediterranean on the rugged Catalonian coast a short distance north of Barcelona. It is home to the Cervera-Guilera family, distributors in Spain of luxury French jeweller Chaumet.

In 2004, they commissioned Barcelona designer Francesc Rifé to design a multi-purpose extension and guest wing for their 1989 two-storey house. A fundamental requirement of the brief was that the annexe be designed in harmony with the existing structure.

The sloping hillside site determined the position of the extension, to the side of the original building; a rear addition was not an option. The clients' decision to add a swimming pool (which was not designed by Rifé) to the property at the same time also influenced its location and its multifunctional nature – the annexe is in regular use as a changing room for the pool.

A key aspect of Rifé's solution to the challenge of aesthetic integration was the addition of a pergola running along the façades of both the new and the old elements, creating a strong and consistent linear bond.

The simple single-storey annexe is built around a frame of concrete. Its five pillars are clad in dark anthracite, a *blanco y negro* contrast with the clean white walls of the original house. Sliding doors minimize the distinction between interior and exterior.

Ipe, a tropical hardwood, has been used for the floor of the external deck, running alongside the pool. The interior is mainly finished in fumé oak panelling and white lacquered hardboard made from wood fibres glued under heat and pressure (MDF).

Internally, the pavilion annexe includes three principal spaces. There is a large open-plan, multi-purpose space – often used as an office – with glass partitions; a gym and attached bathroom with built-in shower; and a bedroom with en-suite dressing-room. The rooms can be used independently or as an integrated whole, depending on need.

A further feature of Rifé's strategy of harmonizing new and old was to make subtle alterations to the façade of the original house, creating external commonalities. The original metalwork and the rolling blinds have been replaced with grey-coloured replicas, picking up the anthracite of the annexe.

Construction of the annexe and completion of the renovations took only five months. The total cost was €270,000 ($338,000).

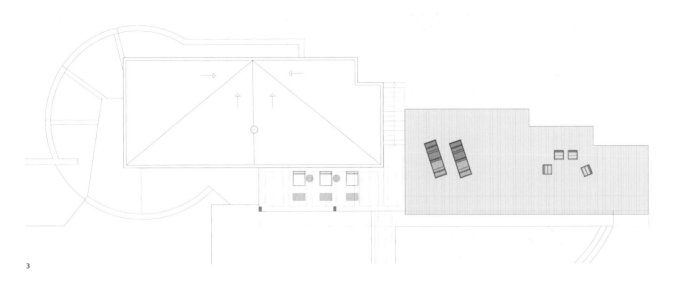

4

3 Roof plan showing the original building on the left and the annexe roof terrace on the right.

4 The annexe includes a gym, double bedroom with en-suite bathroom and shower-room.

5 Fumé oak panelling and white lacquered MDF have been used to finish the interior.

6 Ground-floor plan of the annexe

The five pillars of the annexe are clad in dark anthracite, a *blanco y negro* contrast with the clean white walls of the original house

5

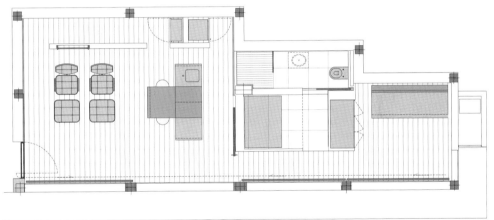

6

1

1 The original nineteenth-century coastguard
station was built in the lee of Dundeady headland,
minimizing wind and sun penetration. The position
of the extension was determined by the ambition to
capture natural light.

2 A cruciform cloister links the two original buildings
– now converted into bedrooms – with the new
glazed wing, which includes the kitchen, dining-room
and communal spaces.

Dirk Cove House

Cork | Ireland | Níall McLaughlin | Space added: 155m² (1,668ft²)

Dirk Cove is an isolated harbour on Ireland's
Atlantic coast. The beautiful yet treacherous
landscape is notorious for shipwrecks
and extreme weather; lighthouses and
coastguard stations line the shore.

The small coastguard station at Dirk
Cove was positioned with an emphasis on
shelter from the elements, to maximize the
number of launches. It was built in the lee
of Dundeady headland to ensure that it was
out of the wind; it was also out of the sun.

This may not have been a problem for
coastguards, men with other priorities,
but access to sunlight would be vital if
the coastguard station was to function
effectively as a private residence. Space
was also limited. The two derelict buildings
– a nineteenth-century farmhouse-style
cottage and a boathouse – were strictly
utilitarian structures. So when Edward
and Anne Fitzmaurice bought the site, the
provision of natural light and living space
were key requirements of the brief.

The Fitzmaurices hired Dublin-born
architect Níall McLaughlin to take on
the challenge. It was a client/architect
relationship with a history – a few years
previously the couple had commissioned
McLaughlin to refurbish their principal home
in Hampstead, London.

McLaughlin's response was to convert
the cottage and the boathouse into the
master bedroom and guest bedrooms
respectively. The kitchen, dining- and sitting-

3 The trapezoidal pavilion reaches out into the ocean;
the roof extends 8 metres (26 feet) over the water.

4 The side wing creates a new courtyard on the
western edge of the site, overlooking the Atlantic.

5 The sleek, white-walled addition is aligned with the
site's geographical grain, which is oriented towards
the south-east.

rooms are located in the new extension, a
sleek, white-walled pavilion with dramatic
roofline projecting towards the ocean. An
asymmetrical cruciform cloister ties the
three buildings together. The arrangement
creates a new courtyard on the western
edge of the site, overlooking the ocean;
a new pathway to the shore has been
integrated into the rebuilt sea-wall, a
safeguard against erosion.

The location and wedge-shaped form
of the timber-framed extension were
determined by the ambition of capturing
light. The addition stretches out towards the
water, away from the growing shadow of
the hill, allowing it to catch the last scraps
of sunlight in the early evening. The western
edge of the pavilion looks out to the ocean
through a floor-to-ceiling window, and its
roof projects 8 metres (26 feet) over the
water.

McLaughlin has furnished the extension
with a rubber floor and a simple concrete
dining-table. Sliding doors offer access to
the courtyard.

The €600,000 ($750,000) extension
was completed in the summer of 2004.
That autumn it survived its first test in the
elements, a one-in-twenty-year storm in
which a Force 10 gale and high spring tide
combined to hurl breakers right up to the
projecting canopy.

5

6 Cross-section looking east

7 Site plan: 1) Parking, 2) Entrance, 3) Dining area in new pavilion, 4) Kitchen, 5) External deck, 6) and 7) services 8) Bedroom, 9) Bedroom, 10) Cloister, 11) Bedroom, 12) Bedroom, 13) New courtyard, 14) Pathway to the shore, 15) enclosed courtyard

8 The visual delicacy of the extension belies its structural strength; the first winter after completion it withstood a Force 10 gale.

Access to sunlight would be vital if the coastguard station was to function effectively as a private residence

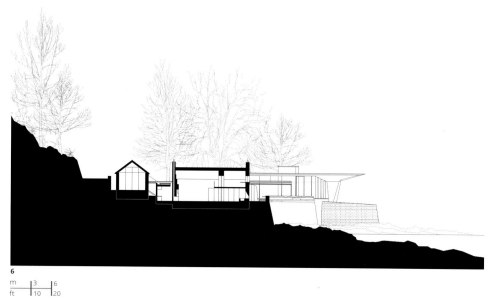

6

m ∣3 ∣6
ft ∣10 ∣20

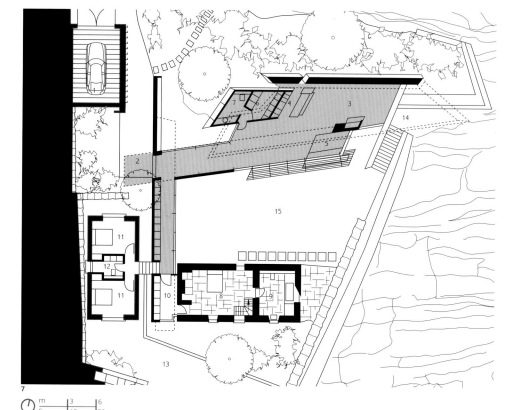

7

m ∣3 ∣6
ft ∣10 ∣20

8

1

1 The zinc entrance/staircase was constructed off-site.
It is attached to the wall at two points.

2 At ground level the front and rear façades were
opened up; circular windows punched into the walls
illuminate the first floor.

3 Architect Pierre Hebbelinck 'reclaimed the original
volume'. All annexes and lean-to additions were
removed. The building was stripped to its bare bones.

Frankfort House

Brussels | Belgium | Atelier d'Architecture Pierre Hebbelinck* SA *Pierre Hebbelinck – Pierre de Wit – Architects

Aline Frankfort is a Belgian creative
consultant and artist. In 2001 she bought
an unremarkable three-storey century-old
house with a double-pitched roof in the
Uccle district of Brussels, an area noted for
its progressive planning department.

At various stages over the years,
annexes and alterations had been grafted
onto the building. The result was a
confusion of cramped internal spaces,
and poor connections between the house
and the irregular-shaped garden. In 2002
Pierre Hebbelinck, an architect best known
for the Museum of Contemporary Arts
at Grand-Hornu in Boussu, Belgium, was
commissioned to make sense of the chaos.

'Madame Frankfort asked for a living
area, an office and an atelier,' explains
Hebbelinck. 'She wanted flowing spaces,
with a black and white colour palette,
so that moving panels would generate a
variety of spatial compositions.'

The brief was to turn a family home
into a living and working space suited to
a cultured consultant with no children.
Hebbelinck decided to strip the building back
to its bones. 'In order to create a simple,
uncluttered space that would meet Madame
Frankfort's needs without the addition of
a new annexe, it was clear that we would
have to reclaim the original volume.'

Every annexe was removed, including a
small shed that formed the front entrance
to the house. Inside, all traces of the former

2

3

4

4 The lightning-bolt-like zinc-coated staircase frees up
space inside the building.

5 Axonometric projection

ceiling, floorboards and window-frames
were erased. 'The outcome was quite
naive, like a house drawn by a child,' says
Hebbelinck. The process also revealed the
original decorative brickwork that had been
concealed as new layers had been added.

At ground level, to emphasize the
strength and solidity of the original building,
Hebbelinck cut away the end walls, thereby
opening up the house to the front and rear
gardens. At the front, three full-height
doors offer views over the lawn; at the rear,
a metal frame supported by two slanted
beams reinforces the sense of transparency
in the ground-level living areas.

On the upper floors, thick cylindrical
glass blocks have been positioned in the
brickwork to create irregularly spaced
lighting effects both inside and outside the
house. A bedroom and bathroom are on the
second floor; the atelier is on the top level.

The most radical alteration, and the
feature that makes the Frankfort house
relevant to this book, is a lightning-bolt-like
extension wrapped in zinc which projects
from the front of the house and runs along
its side. It occupies the same position as the
pre-existing entrance 'shed'.

The independent structure was brought
to site in one piece. It encloses the entrance
and staircase, offering access to every level
and leaving the internal spaces free for
other uses. To break down the zinc mass,
Hebbelinck designed it to 'float' above the
ground. It is supported on a 4-centimetre
(1.6-inch) steel rod at the bottom and hangs
from a beam at the top.

The total cost of the renovation and
extension was €125,000 ($160,000). The
work took two years to complete – 12
months to design and 12 months to build.

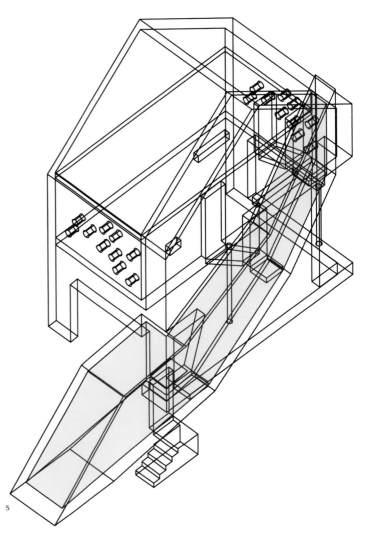

5

6 Aline Frankfort, a creative consultant, specified a colour palette of black and white for the first floor atelier.

7 Moving panels create a range of spatial compositions.

8 Mirrors on the panels allow areas to be partially closed off while still bouncing light from one end of the house to the other.

9 Rear elevation

10 Front elevation

11 Side elevation

6

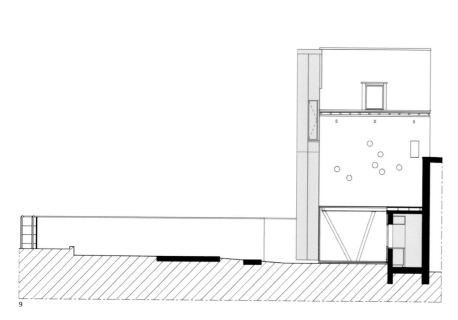

9

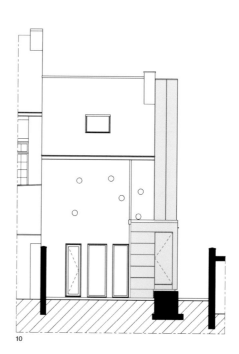

10

7

8

The brief was to turn a family home into a live/work space suited to a cultured consultant with no children

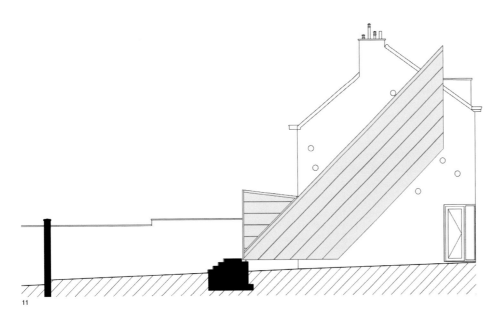

11

1 The original two-storey farmhouse is situated in the beautiful Natural Park of the Vulcanic Area de la Garrotxa.

2 As well as adding the bedroom annexe, the architects overhauled the farmhouse and improved circulation.

Country houses are free from the stylistic constraints of fashionable urban centres. They are aesthetically neutral playgrounds for innovation. At least that's how architect Jordi Hidalgo of Hidalgo Hartmann explains the asymmetrical steel-clad bedroom annexe for a century-old stone-built country estate at the end of a valley in rural Girona.

The bedroom was only one part of the design challenge. Client Lluis and Montserrat also commissioned the architects to design a circulation space, partially located underground, to unite the three disparate components of the property – the main house, a small stone hut and the new annexe – at ground level. The three volumes remain separated at first-floor level, an arrangement typical of country houses in the region.

The circulation hall occupies a deep void, the foundations of a building long since removed. To allow natural light into the space Hidalgo created a soft ramp on the south side.

As well as a large bedroom, the abstract cabaña (cabin) annexe contains a bathroom and a dressing-room. It was designed as a private space; the only means of access is via a staircase leading from the new distribution hall.

Hidalgo Hartmann describes the extension as 'an abstract container enclosed within steel sheets of different dimensions, recalling the way farmers used to construct their sheds'. Three large windows reveal the beautiful rolling views of the Natural Park of the Vulcanic Area de la Garrotxa.

The cabaña sits in a steel structural frame and is supported on a foundation

New Cabaña

Girona | Spain | Hidalgo Hartmann | Space added: 200m² (2,152ft²)

3

3 A soft ramp on the south side allows natural light to flood into the circulation hall.

4 Ground floor plan.

5 The partially subterranean hallway occupies the foundations of a building long since removed.

of 300-millimetre (11.8-inch) reinforced concrete walls. It is clad entirely in 3-millimetre (1/8-inch) steel sheets weathered to give a rust-like appearance (Cor-ten). The interior is finished with white-painted walls, exposed local stone and dark sucupira wood.

With a total budget of €180,000 ($225,000) Hidalgo Hartmann added 200 square metres (2,152 square feet) of space to the estate.

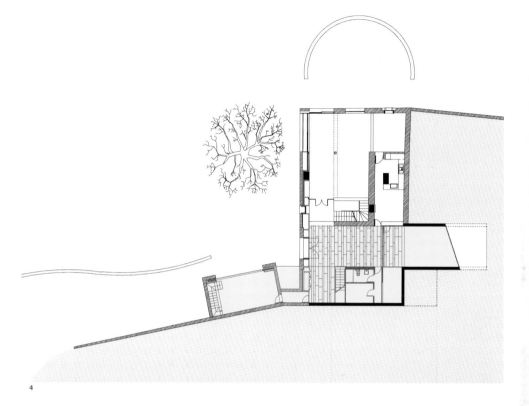

4

5

6

7

Hidalgo Hartmann describes the extension as, 'an abstract container enclosed within steel sheets of different dimensions, recalling the way farmers used to construct their sheds'

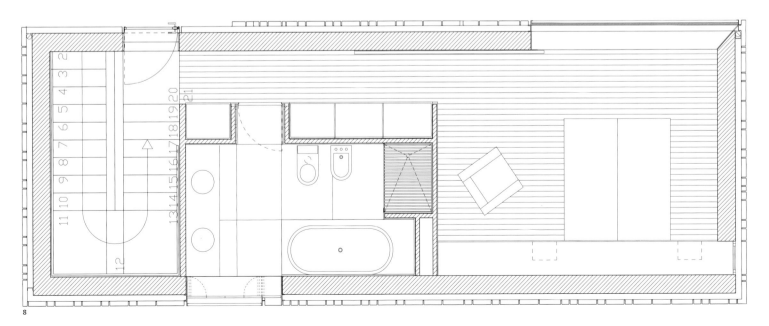

8

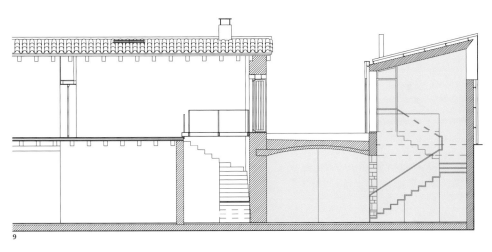

6 The asymmetrical 'cabaña' is enclosed within Corten sheets of different shapes and sizes, a striking contrast to the elegant brickwork of the original.

7 The cabaña comprises a bedroom, bathroom and dressing area.

8 Plan of the first-floor bedroom

9 Cross section looking south

10 Large windows frame views of the rolling hills.

9

10

1

1 A clean, light and well-organized family home has evolved from a badly ventilated and dark 'ranch house'.

2 The original 1956 structure related poorly to its site; views of the Santa Ynez Mountains and the Pacific Ocean were blocked.

Santa Barbara Ranch House

Santa Barbara | California | USA | Nick Noyes Architecture | Space added: approximately 50m² (538ft²)

Film-maker Richard Dallett and his wife, Lloyd, who is an artist, lived for many years in Brooklyn, thriving in New York's creative industries, but after the birth of their daughter the city no longer held quite the same appeal. Lloyd Dallett, who went to school in California, began hankering for a return to the climate, space and pace of life out West. With flexible careers and friends in Santa Barbara, the Dalletts made the move in 2001.

Their ambition was to find a house that was close to the town, with potential for development and views of the Pacific Ocean. What they found was a much neglected 1956 ranch house with a pitched roof in the suburb of Mission Canyon. It had views – the Santa Ynez Mountains on one side and the Pacific on the other – but they were obscured by foliage and the illogical orientation of the house.

San Francisco architect Nick Noyes was commissioned to renovate and enlarge the property. 'The existing 135-square-metre [1,450-square-foot] house was too small,' he says. 'It also failed to take advantage of the exceptional climate and did not utilize the site in a meaningful way.'

Having first repaired the foundations and installed plumbing and electricity, Noyes removed two small rooms on the far side of the building. This opened up a long space in the heart of the house, with views over the garden, which is used as the living- and

2

3 Site plan: 1) Studio, 2) Master bedroom, 3) Kitchen,
  4) Living/dining-room, 5) Bedroom, 6) Office,
  7) Terrace, 8) Lawn

4 The new raised roof allows light into the house and
  increases the height of the ceilings.

5 The enclosed external patio.

dining-room. But its role goes further than
that. The space attracts light and ventilation
from all sides, opens up views to the south,
north and east and glues together all the
internal and external spaces that lead from
it. Noyes thinks of it as the 'town square'.

On the south side, the square opens onto
an enclosed external patio. On the north,
a barn-style sliding door screens a built-in
work area and bookcase and conceals the
corridor to one of the bedrooms. The 50-
square-metre (538-square-foot) extension,
which incorporates an office, spare bedroom
and bathroom, defines the south-east
corner of the house.

Noyes originally planned to build a
two-storey tower as the extension, to
optimize views. But neighbours rejected the
idea. Instead, he designed a single-storey
structure that blends stylistically with the
rest of the house – it has a sloping ceiling,
a neutral colour scheme, an abundance
of exposed timber for warmth, and large
windows to allow natural light in.

The other major alteration was the
conversion of the former double garage
next to the entrance into a studio for Lloyd
Dallett.

The overall effect is a clean, integrated
light-filled family home – a far cry from the
decaying shack from which it evolved.

3

4

5

'The existing house failed to take advantage of the exceptional climate and did not utilize the site in a meaningful way'

6

6 The large living/dining area, known as the 'town square', replaces two small rooms. It plays a vital role in family life, uniting the exterior with all the internal rooms.

7 The new wing, which includes an office, spare bedroom and bathroom, defines the south-east corner of the house.

7

1

2

1 The original two-storey detached house was an anonymous cog in Dortmund's suburban wheel.

2 An additional 57 square metres (614 square feet) of liveable floor space is accommodated inside the extension. It includes two nurseries, a bedroom and a bathroom.

3 Overlooking the road, the dark-stained monolithic extension has transformed the identity of the house.

Villa 57+

Dortmund | Germany | ArchiFactory.de | Space added: 57m² (614ft²)

Architects Matthias Herrmann and Matthias Koch of ArchiFactory.de like to keep their work simple, albeit with an 'architectural' twist. Since 1999, the Bochum-based team has dedicated itself to the development of 'architecture based on no external visible sign'. Their work is often described as 'sculptural' and 'monolithic'.

An early example was the Ebeling House (completed 2001), a cuboid extension to a 1940s Dortmund house that they clad in silver-grey larch. The pared-down finish avoided all extraneous detail; there were no gutters, eaves or chimneys. The extension to Villa 57+, also in Dortmund, continues Herrmann and Koch's meditation on residential monoliths.

The brief required the expansion of an inconspicuous two-storey detached house with a pitched roof. Two nurseries, a bedroom and a bathroom were needed to accommodate the growing Köppen family. Hermann and Koch were also commissioned to design a dressing-room in the existing house.

The client was open to ideas about the placement of the extension, although it was specified that it must not impose on woodland to the east of the site. After considering the options, Herrmann and Koch decided to tack the additional space onto the road-facing end of the house.

At first sight the extension resembles a Monopoly house: it is angular, devoid of features and appears to have been picked up and placed alongside another property. Closer inspection reveals that the new slice of house is actually clad all over in finely detailed dark-stained Douglas fir boards laid vertically over the timber frame. A window and skylight also become apparent, but there is no entrance – access is via the original house. It is all a stark contrast with the conventional white stucco and anthracite tiles of the original.

The intention was to design the extension in sympathy with the woodland setting, but to make it obviously distinct from the original house. As well as the selection of materials, and minimal uses of architectural features, this has been achieved by projecting the roof of the extension up, pointing towards the road. The walls also splay outwards from the existing house. It is an exercise in asymmetry.

The effect is both enigmatic and highly stylized. The unpromisingly bland suburban context serves only to enhance its unexpected beauty.

Internally, the nurseries are located on the ground floor, with the bathroom and bedroom on the floor above.

The work cost €90,000 ($115,000), and took just over a year from design to completion.

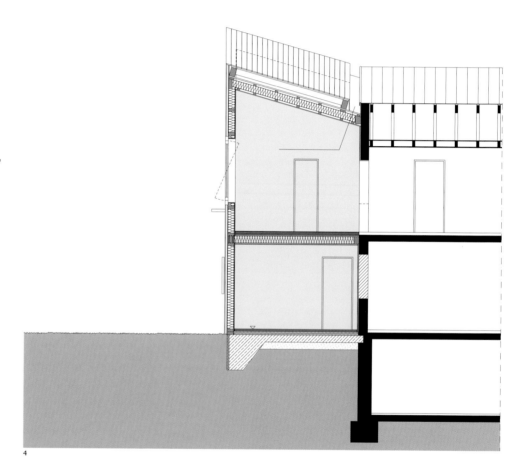

4

The intention was to design the extension in sympathy with the woodland setting, but to make it obviously distinct from the original house

5

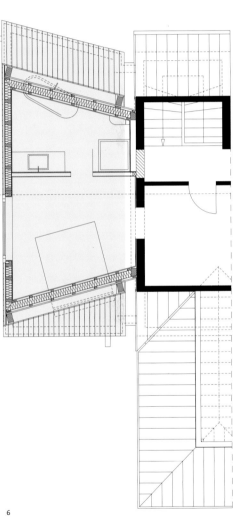

6

chapter 4
Outdoors

1

2

m
ft
|1
|5
|2
|3
|10

1 The Japanese-style sunken garden is intimately connected with the living- and dining-rooms. Irregular slates are a visual link with the sunken and patio gardens.

2 Cross-section looking west: the 1960s house covers three storeys, the lowest of which is entirely underground. On the north it is two storeys, with the voluminous lower level partially submerged.

3 The stainless-steel staircase links the sunken garden with the patio garden above. It is supported by the sidewall, creating the impression that it is floating.

Dr Gabka House

Munich | Germany | Landau + Kindelbacher Architekten | Space added: swimming pool 24.6m² (265 square feet); south-facing deck 70 sm² (753ft²); sunken garden 17.6m² (189ft²)

Architects often talk about 'breaking down the distinction between outside and inside'; it was one of the fundamental tenets of Modernism. In the world of residential alterations, this typically finds expression in a sliding or bi-fold door inserted in a rear kitchen extension, facilitating fluid access to the garden. But there are occasions when it is the external areas, not the house, that require attention in improving the interaction between inside and outside.

Dr Christian Gabka bought this three-storey pitched-roof 1960s house from a painter. It was in good condition, but poorly connected with the large, under-utilized garden that surrounds it on three sides. The other difficulty was that some of the internal spaces were dark, and the lower ground floor was inconveniently configured.

The former studio was particularly problematic. Located on the north side of the property, it was partially submerged. The gloomy light might have suited the painter, but it was insufficient for use in a dining- and living-room, Gabka's intended use for the space.

Architects Gerhard Landau and Ludwig Kindelbacher cleared the small sunken garden outside the studio and dug it out to create space for a Japanese-style courtyard garden. They planted it with a maple tree and low-growing shrubs so as not to block the light that floods the interior through full-height glass walls.

3

4 A short staircase leads from the entrance lobby into the former painter's studio, which is partially underground.

5 A half-height partition wall divides the former painting studio into living and dining areas without blocking light from the full-height windows.

The highlight of the sunken garden is a prefabricated steel staircase that leads to the patio garden above, emphasizing the point that circulation around the house is not restricted to the interior. The staircase is welded to a side sheet that is attached to the wall, creating the impression that it is floating in mid-air. Its structural strength is derived from the folds of the metal.

Alterations to the exterior space were only half the challenge. Work was also carried out on the former studio. Once it had been gutted, a half-height partition wall was inserted to separate the dining area from the lounge, and the large volume was painted white to attract light. The effect is a bright, airy living space, intimately connected with the sunken garden.

The largest feature of the commission to overhaul the house was redesigning the south-facing garden, including the addition of a large timber terrace and a new swimming pool. A jacuzzi and a small terrace were built in the patio garden.

The theme of integrating internal and external spaces also influenced the inclusion of a steel-framed balcony that cantilevers out from the upper level of the southern façade. When shut, a cloth sunscreen creates a completely enclosed outside space.

4

5

6 The south-facing timber deck and integrated swimming pool were the largest elements of the commission to overhaul the house.

7 A new steel-framed balcony projects from the upper floor on the southern façade, further blurring the boundaries between interior and exterior. When shut, a cloth sunscreen creates an enclosed external space.

7

The house was poorly connected with the large garden. The other difficulty was that some of the internal spaces were dark

1

Duane Street Live/Work Space

New York | USA | Marpillero Pollak Architects | Space created: external space 28m² (300ft²)

2

Number 132 Duane Street in Manhattan's Tribeca district was originally one of a group of three nineteenth-century industrial manufacturing buildings. Today, substantially altered, it is the only survivor.

The other two buildings were victims of the widening of nearby Church Street in the 1920s to facilitate the open-pit construction of the Eighth Avenue Subway. By the late 1990s, Number 132 was in an advanced state of decay, and might have suffered a similar fate but for the fact that it was protected as part of the area's historic fabric.

Architects Linda Pollak and Sandro Marpillero acquired the building in order to adapt it as a three-storey sequence of living and working spaces. Their alterations and additions have retained the structure's heroic industrial dimensions – the original bays were each 8 metres (26 feet) wide – while simultaneously managing to create a garden and infuse the interior with natural light.

The work involved the removal of portions of the first floor and backyard to create an enclosed courtyard that overlooks a back garden through a dramatic window 3 metres (10 feet) wide and 8 metres (26 feet) high. It has brought the once dark, dank basement into full-time use.

The landscaped west-facing garden is a combination of vegetation and light-reflecting white river stone. To maximize

The alterations have retained the structure's heroic dimensions, while simultaneously creating a garden and infusing the interior with natural light

3

3 The hard-landscaped garden is visible from the enclosed courtyard through a 3-metre-by-8-metre (10-foot-by-26-foot) window that floods the three-storey building with natural light.

4 Garden level floor plan: 1) Garden, 2) Living area, 3) Bar, 4) Kitchen, 5) Office, 6) Shop

5 The red dotted line indicates the portion of the first floor removed to create living space; the yellow line indicates the portion of the yard removed to clear space for the garden.

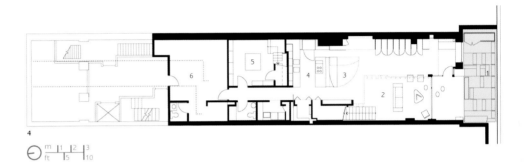

4

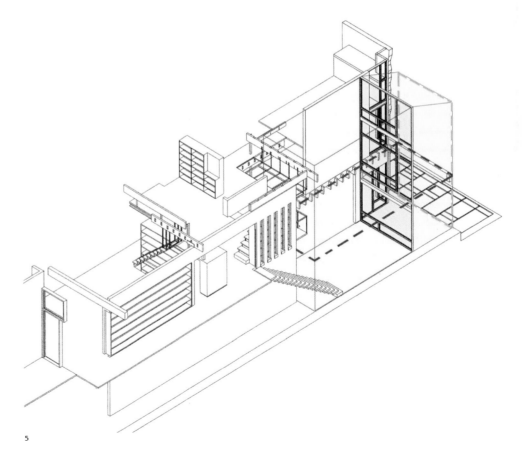

5

the levels of daylight, Pollak and Marpillero
fixed angled mirrors to an adjacent building,
reflecting strips of sky and cloud into their
property.

Internally the building has been arranged
so that work and living spaces are combined
on three levels – the basement, ground floor
and mezzanine – with the office at the front
facing the street. Corridors, the stairwell
and strategically placed bookcases mediate
between work and living spaces – the office
stair-bookshelf extends from basement to
mezzanine, shifting from solid below to
transparent above.

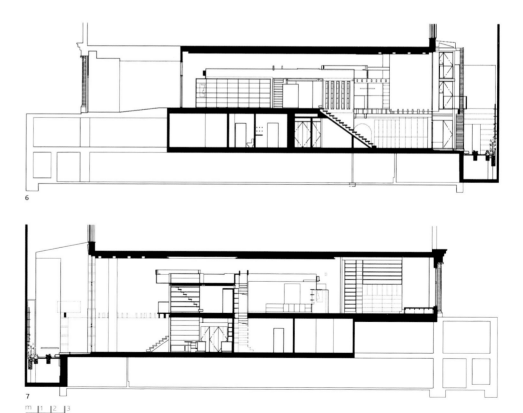

6

7

m |1 |2 |3
ft |5 |10

1 Cross-section looking east

2 Floor plan

3 The terrace opens up spectacular views of the Manhattan skyline.

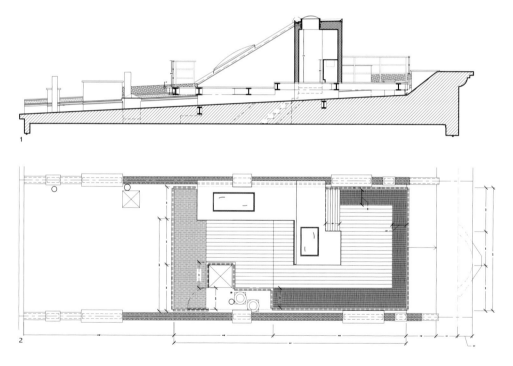

1

2

Roof-terraces have never been so popular, particularly in dense urban areas. The reasons are both economic – sky-high property values mean that traditional gardens are increasingly the preserve of the well-heeled, and practical – the relative ease of maintaining a roof garden suits the lifestyles of workaholic urban professionals. Planted roof-terraces also improve the urban ecological balance and provide an additional layer of insulation. Perhaps best of all, they can add value to a property: by as much as 10–15 per cent in major Western urban centres.

Stefania Rinaldi designed this roof-terrace as part of a commission to integrate the recently acquired top floor of a brownstone townhouse on the Upper West Side with the rest of the apartment. Previously, the roof had been accessible only for maintenance and the fire escape.

It was a property Rinaldi already knew, having combined the third and fourth storeys into a coherent whole a year previously. In fact, she was familiar with the whole building: in 2003 she had renovated the ground- and lower-ground-floor apartment of the same building for a Swedish couple.

The Joabar family's brief for the roof-terrace was for a private green oasis and cooking facilities for al fresco dining. It went without saying that the scheme should optimize views of the New York skyline.

Manhattan roof-terrace

New York │ USA │ Studio Rinaldi │ Space added: 40m^2 (430ft^2)

4 A new staircase from the remodelled fifth floor provides access to the terrace.

5 The rooflight over the bend of the staircase.

6 The new stucco stair enclosure also houses a refrigerator and sink, for barbecues and al fresco dining.

7 Planted roof-terraces improve the urban ecological balance and provide an additional layer of insulation.

4   5

6

There were also practical planning issues to consider. The building is protected by New York City's Landmarks Preservation Commission, which meant that the terrace had to be set back 0.6 metres (2 feet) from the edge, to ensure that it is not visible from the ground. In addition, fire regulations required the use of fire-retardant wood, which led Rinaldi to use a perforated galvanized-steel grille around the perimeter. The grille also works as a drain for planting.

The terrace itself is split over two levels. Both are decked, to help spread the load. The slope and height of the existing party walls determined the location of the structural beams and the level of the new terrace. A fibreglass railing encloses the space and does not obscure the views.

The terrace is accessed from the fifth-floor living-room via a new dog-leg staircase. A window positioned over the 90-degree bend lets light into the interior. On the terrace itself, a new stucco-clad stair enclosure creates a monolithic sculptural rooftop feature. Irene Joabar uses the terrace every day: 'After a hectic day at work, I recharge myself spending time on the roof, tending the garden while sipping a glass of wine and watching the sunset.'

Roof-terraces might look simple and cheap enough, but the cost of a good-quality space made with durable materials can easily mount – the Joabars' cost in the region of $100,000. Perhaps the main reason for the cost is that roof-terraces are constantly exposed to wind, rain and sun. In such conditions, substandard materials degrade quickly.

7

1

1 'Winking eye' sculptures on the roof-terrace extension lend presence to the façade, and help to align the building with its three-storey neighbours. The use of zinc and steel refers to the area's industrial past.

2 The 1960s structure was built as a timber merchant's depot and converted into a driving school before becoming a private home.

3 The ground floor of the remodelled and extended house is dedicated to the children, the first floor to communal family life, and the roof-terrace to the adults.

Terrace and swimming pool

Nantes | France | Mûrisserie Parent-Rachdi | Space added: roof-terrace 60m² (646ft²)

It is hard to believe that this three-storey family house was once a timber depot in the heart of Nantes' industrial district. The building has been extended and completely transformed by architects and owners Yves Parent and Sonia Rachdi.

The original two-storey concrete structure dates from the 1960s. It was built on the foundations of an industrial warehouse; for decades the area between the River Loire and the main railway station of Nantes was a thriving commercial quarter. The building served two purposes: as a storage depot for timber, and as a staff car-park.

The building went up just as the curtain was coming down on the Ile de Nantes' period of industrial potency, and some time in the 1970s it was sold to a driving school. Only very minor alterations were required to adapt it to its new function: a small reception area was created on the ground floor, and the upper-storey offices were turned into a private apartment; the ground-level garages required no attention at all.

The building's third incarnation, as a family home, came about when Parent and Rachdi bought the property in 2002. The timing coincided with a scheme to regenerate the Ile de Nantes as a mixed-use urban quarter.

The challenge of turning a public building into a private home was accentuated by

2

3

4 Plan of the first-floor living area

5 A mosaic of coloured glass surrounds the swimming
   pool in the enclosed courtyard garden.

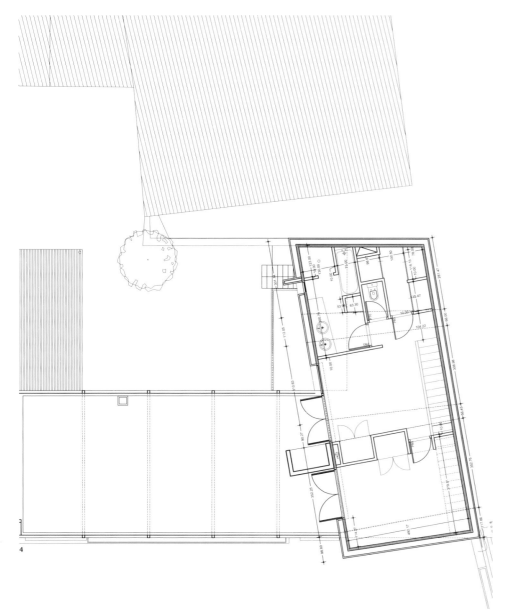

4

these plans. 'At the moment the street is
a cul-de-sac, but within a few years it will
be a grand urban boulevard,' explain Parent
and Rachdi.

The retouched 1960s façade projects
a message of private yet light-hearted
domesticity. At ground level full-height slit
windows have replaced the garage doors.
On the upper levels steel balustrades and
zinc sculptures reminiscent of Salvador Dali's
'winking eyes' refer to the area's industrial
heritage.

Access to the outdoors was a
fundamental feature of the design
approach, as was the organization of the
house into zones for the children, the
parents and communal family life.

The former garages on the ground floor
have been converted into self-contained
en suite bedrooms linked by a corridor. All
of them have access to the new swimming
pool, the centrepiece of the enclosed
courtyard garden, a play-space designed for
the children and their friends.

The first floor contains all the common
areas, including the kitchen, the dining-
room, the living-room and a small library.
The Juliet balcony on the front façade and
the small timber terrace to the rear required
only minor modifications.

The new top-storey roof-terrace is
dedicated to the adults. It is a place for
relaxation and solitude. It also has fantastic
views in all directions, and ensures that the
roof height is aligned with the adjacent
three-storey building.

6

The challenge of turning a public building into a private
home was accentuated by plans to turn the Ile de Nantes
into a mixed-use urban quarter

6 A new staircase links the communal living spaces on the first floor with the 'adults only' roof-terrace.

7 On the ground floor former garages have been converted into bedrooms.

7

chapter 5

Innovative
additions

1

1 The rooftop apartment optimizes the views and fresh air of Mexico City's elevated Tecamachalco district.

2 Pre-Hispanic vegetation, mushroom-like acrylic stools and a lava mosaic combine to eclectic effect on the terrace.

Casa pR34

Mexico City | Mexico | Rojkind Arquitectos | Space added: 136m² (1,464ft²)

Choreography and youthful Latin passion underpinned the design of this rooftop apartment, but the curvaceous composition was only the visible element of a commission to refurbish and extend a 1968 concrete house in hilly Tecamachalco, one of Mexico City's more desirable districts, where the air is fresh and the views panoramic.

In 2001, the client – who prefers to remain anonymous – invited his friend Michel Rojkind (a former rock drummer) of Rojkind Arquitectos, to propose designs to enhance the sense of space within the original house. This led to subtle enhancements of the concrete-framed prow and double-height living-room, and improvements to the access and circulation. The other main alteration involved strengthening the house to carry the weight of a rooftop apartment, which the client wanted as a present for his dancer daughter.

For the apartment, Rojkind took inspiration from its occupant's profession and personality. It was designed to resemble two dancers in motion; the colour red symbolizes her youth and passion.

The apartment sits on and is anchored by a black steel frame, recessed beneath it to create the impression that it is floating on the roof. Steel I-beams frame the volume; steel sheets form the shell. To accommodate the expansion and contraction of the metal in the powerful Mexican sun, the shell was first primed and then coated in plastic paint.

3 A screen allows the kitchen to be shut away from the living area. White-painted chipboard walls accentuate the space and light in the column-free interior.

3

Steel-workers from a local panel-beating firm were hired to help build the frame. Rojkind was impressed by their capacity to improvise. 'In other parts of the world this would have cost a lot of money . . . but these are the kinds of thing you can do in Mexico,' he says.

At the entry the 136-square-metre (1,464-square-foot) apartment is divided into two halves on separate levels. The upper level contains a large open-plan dining and seating area with attached kitchen; a curtain can be drawn to screen the kitchen from the rest of the space. A second reception area and the bedroom are located on the lower level. White-painted chipboard lines the walls, making the most of the light and the column-free volumes.

The lower level also overlooks the roof-terrace, which has an almost lunar-landscape-like quality. Chips of lava left over from the cladding of the main house have been used to create a mosaic floor; transparent acrylic stools mark the position of skylights. Rojkind also found space for some pre-Hispanic plants. The vegetation softens the rock face, which was excavated to create space for the apartment.

It was stipulated that the existing house and the apartment be independent of each other. In terms of power provision and plumbing this presented few problems. Access was more of a challenge. Rojkind's solution was to design separate exits from the enclosed ground-level garage, the rooftop being reached via a spiral staircase.

The apartment was designed and built in only eight months.

4 The rounded edges of the steel frame introduce a hint of sensuality and soften the hard steel shell.

5 A steel frame clad in steel plates creates the fluid forms of the split-level apartment.

6 Floor plan: 1) Entrance, 2) Living space, 3) Seating area, 4) Kitchen, 5) Dining area, 6) Toilet, 7) Bedroom, 8) Storage, 9) Bathroom

7 The form of the penthouse was inspired by the personality and profession of the owner's daughter, a young ballet dancer.

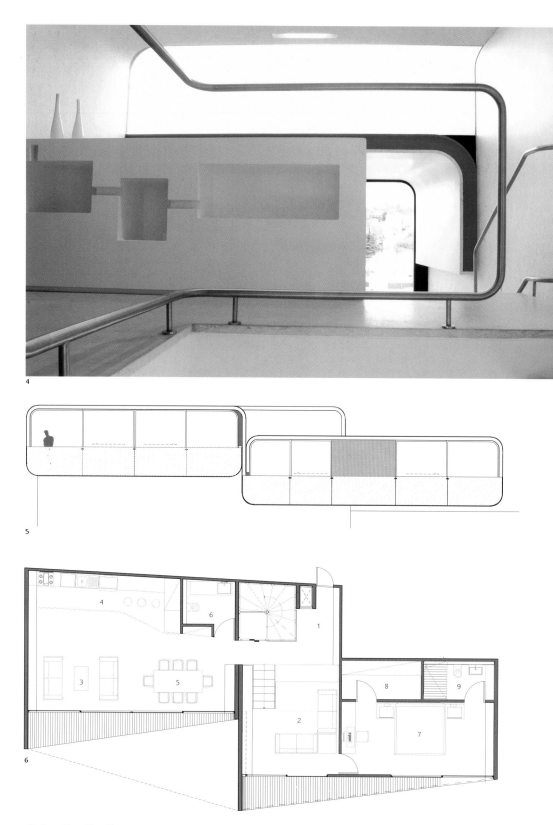

4

5

6

m
ft
1
5
2
3
10

The other main alteration involved strengthening the house to carry the weight of a rooftop apartment, which the client wanted as a present for his ballet-dancer daughter

1

1   Extensions to existing buildings are the only type
of construction permitted in the Glaskogen Nature
Reserve in south-west Sweden.

2   Aside from an internal refit the original nineteenth-
century fisherman's cabin was left untouched.

Dragspelhuset (Accordion House)

Lake Övre Gla | Sweden | 24H Architecture | Space added: 30m² (323ft²); 48m² (517ft²) when fully extended

Planning regulations in Sweden's Glaskogen Nature Reserve prohibit the construction of new buildings on the shore of Lake Övre Gla. If you need more space, the only option available is to buy an existing structure and add an extension to it. This was the approach taken by Dutch architect couple Maartje Lammers and Boris Zeisser, who bought a 15-square-metre (161-square-foot) nineteenth-century fisherman's cabin and turned it into a holiday home for themselves and their daughter.

The exterior of the hut was left untouched. Its conversion into a bedroom required only improved insulation and the removal of antiquated internal features. The bulk of Lammers and Zeisser's time was devoted to the creation of a playful yet practical extension to the south-east of the sloping woodland site.

Even when stretching the planning regulations to the limit, Lammers and Zeisser were only able to extend the cabin by 30 square metres (323 square feet). Thinking around the problem, they realized that they could add more space as long as it did not touch the ground. It was this challenge, allied to a long-standing interest in designing buildings that evolve, whether through a season or through a day – hence the name of their practice, 24H Architecture – that led to the extraordinary extendable annexe.

2

The amorphous structure is built around a plywood frame and clad in low-maintenance weather-resistant red cedar shingle imported from Canada; all other materials were sourced locally. The really clever part is that it sits on a timber frame that can itself be extended.

Depending on the weather, the season or the number of guests in the house, the north-eastern end, which is next to the stream, slides out like a matchbox to add an extra 18 square metres (194 square feet) of space to the house. It is this action that lends the house its name: Dragspelhuset is Swedish for 'the Accordion House'.

The extendable section sits on timber beams 50 centimetres by 20 centimetres by 9 metres (20 inches by 8 inches by 30 feet). It takes one person a matter of minutes to extend the Accordion. A few turns of a handle are all that is required to activate the simple and inexpensive system of ropes and pulleys.

When compressed, the addition accommodates a dining area, a living-room and a kitchen. When fully extended, the kitchen doubles in size, a floor-to-ceiling window reveals views of the lake, and the living-room cantilevers out over the stream that forms the boundary of the site. At its far end, a chimney emits smoke from the wood-burning stove below, and an eye-like porthole overlooks the stream-fed open-air hot tub. The effect is of a scaly elephant with an erect trunk.

The interior of the retractable element of the extension is lined in reindeer hides, a lesson learned from the indigenous Sámi people of northern Scandinavia and the

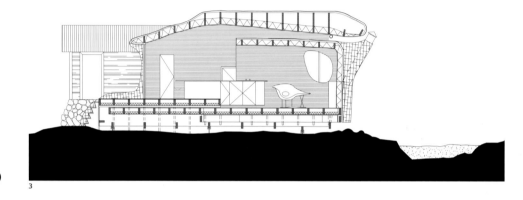

3

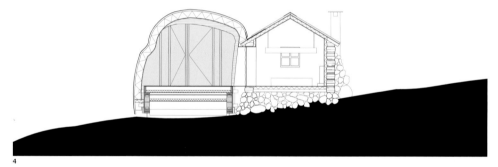

4

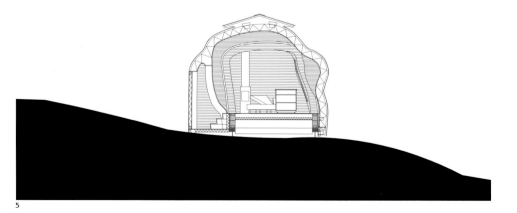

5

6

A chimney emits smoke from the wood-burning stove below, and an eye-like porthole overlooks the open-air hot tub. The effect is of a scaly elephant with an erect trunk

7 The organic shape of the extension blends with the woodland setting.

8 Red cedar shingle wrapped around a plywood frame create the extension's biomorphic appearance.

9 The 'Accordion' can be extended in a matter of minutes; a few turns of a handle are all that is required to activate the simple system of ropes and pulleys.

Kola Peninsula. In the warmer months, when the annexe is in its extended 'summer' format, the hides block out heat during the day and retain it at night. In its compressed 'winter' format, the double-walled extension becomes a super-insulated cocoon.

Despite its apparent structural complexity, the Accordion House is a low-tech, low-impact building. Solar panels provide all almost the power needed for the lights, and cooking is done on a small gas-powered stove. Given the beautiful, wild setting, it is also suitably basic. The toilet does not have a septic tank – it is difficult to obtain consent in the nature reserve – and the bath is a stream-fed outdoor hot tub.

The total cost of the refurbishment to the fisherman's cabin and the construction of the Accordion annexe was €80,000 ($100,000).

7

8

1

1 The modular portable home has been designed to occupy flat roofs on top of high-rise buildings in city centres worldwide.

2 The Loftcube encloses 40 square metres (430 square feet) of flexible floor space, including a bathroom, bedroom and kitchen.

Loftcube

Germany | Studio Aisslinger | Space added: 40m² (430ft²)

2

Loftcube is an instant penthouse, a prefabricated residential module designed to occupy flat roofs in dense urban areas. Since 2003 a prototype of the concept has occupied the top of the Universal Music building in Berlin and of the Galeries Lafayette in Paris.

The idea was developed by Werner Aisslinger of German architecture and design practice Studio Aisslinger. His ambition is to use the roofs of post-Second-World-War high-rise buildings to provide young professionals with accommodation in city centres around the world, a prospect that might otherwise be beyond their means – a new Loftcube costs €55,000–70,000 ($70,000–87,500) to buy and install.

Aisslinger envisages the model appealing both to owner-occupiers and to tenants. He explains: 'To promote ownership the weight of the cubes has been calculated to allow transport by freight helicopter or construction crane. Alternatively the modular shell can be dismantled and transported in sections, which is much cheaper.'

Not every rooftop will be able to accommodate a Loftcube. Each of the steel-framed cuboid volumes – the dimensions are 6.6 metres by 6.6 metres by 3 metres (21 foot 8 inches by 21 foot 8 inches by 9 feet 10 inches) – weighs around 2.5 tonnes, a load spread between stilts 4 metres (13 feet 10 inches) high. This is sufficient

3 A 'functional panel' with integrated shower and plant basins separates the bathroom and living areas; the showerhead is manœuvrable to both sides.

4 With the sliding walls retracted, the Loftcube becomes one large living space.

3

to withstand wind drag, but potentially overbearing for the host building.

Power and access also need consideration. Loftcubes are dependent on their hosts for electricity, plumbing and stairwells or lifts. Assuming that these requirements can be accommodated, the only other preparatory factor is to secure the perimeter of the roof with railings. Once everything is in place it is estimated that a team of three people can erect a Loftcube in two to four days.

Loftcubes provide a floor area of approximately 40 square metres (430 square feet), subdivided into a bathroom, a kitchen and an open-plan living and sleeping space that occupies approximately two-thirds of the total area. Sliding panels on tracks define the spatial divisions.

Aisslinger made his name as a furniture designer for companies including Cappellini and Interlubke. His expertise is evident in the space-efficient arrangement of the internal fittings of the Loftcube. For instance, the panel between the kitchen and the bathroom features an integrated tap that can be manoeuvred to either side for use in both the kitchen sink and the washbasin.

The shower head in the functional panel that separates the living area from the bathroom works along similar lines; the faucet can be manoeuvred to either the shower on one side or the pot-plants on the other.

Owners or tenants can customize Loftcubes to their own requirements. External finishes can be selected from a palette of materials of different colours and translucency. For the prototype, Studio Aisslinger used plastic glazing and timber louvres to clad approximately 70 per cent

5 A palette of cladding and glazing materials allows owners to personalize their own Loftcube and minimize glare.

6 Sliding panels on tracks subdivide the kitchen and bathroom from the main living space.

of the volume, with white laminated lightweight moulded plastic (Polystyrol) making up the balance. Other options include timber and plastic laminates, solid timber and acrylic sheets.

6

1 The weight of the portable parasite is carried by thick steel cables slung over the roof of the host building and anchored on the other side. A structural engineer's report is required to confirm the strength of every host building.

2 The prototype was originally strapped to the side of a former cotton mill in Leipzig (far right). It has since been positioned in the centre of Cologne (right), exactly the type of dense urban setting for which it was designed.

Claustrophobia was the catalyst for the Rucksack House. During spells living in cramped flats in New York and London, Munich sculptor Stefan Eberstadt dreamt about space. 'Some of these apartments had only one window. I'd look out of them and imagine the space in front as a real walk-in room,' he explains. On his return to Germany he got to work. The prototype was first installed in Leipzig in 2004.

As its name implies, the Rucksack House is a portable structure that is suspended from a host building which carries its weight on straps, in this case thick steel cables which run over the roof and are anchored on the opposite side. Four metal spikes positioned on the open side of the cube slip into holes drilled in the façade of the host, fixing it in position. A crane is required to lift the room into place. The process takes only a few hours.

Planning consent takes a little longer, and before this can be considered, a structural engineer's report on the suitability of the host building must be compiled. The project is then at the mercy of the local planners, many of whom it can be assumed will not previously have been confronted with a portable parasite strapped to the side of a building.

To date Eberstadt has convinced planners in Leipzig and Cologne of the Rucksack's

1

Rucksack House

Germany │ **Stefan Eberstadt** │ **Space added: 9m² (97ft²)**

2

3

3 A crane is required to lift the prefabricated Rucksack House into position. The process takes only a few hours.

4 Exterior-grade plywood with a dark absorbent resin was used to clad the prototype, but the cube can be re-clad or painted to suit its setting.

5 Axonometric projection

merits. In Leipzig, it was suspended from a former cotton mill, above a canal. It stayed in position for a year, as part of an exhibition titled 'Xtreme Houses'.

The precedent encouraged the authorities in Cologne to grant consent for the Rucksack House to be attached to the side of a 1960s office and residential block. 'That was a really good position. It was right in the centre of the city, where space is tight: exactly the kind of constricted location that it was designed for,' says Eberstadt.

To date, the Rucksack House has not been trialled outside Germany, but Eberstadt has received a steady stream of interest from around the world. The challenge is to build the cubes in sufficient numbers to bring the cost down; Eberstadt thinks that it should be possible to reduce the cost to around €27,000 ($34,000), exclusive of installation. At the time of writing he was looking for a backer.

With an area of 9 square metres (97 square feet), the steel-framed cube is a decent-sized room. Eberstadt designed it as a bolthole with minimal furnishings; it could equally be used as a bedroom or study – power and telephone cables can be tapped from the host.

The exterior of the prototype is a red shade of brown, but it could be painted or re-clad in any colour to suit its setting. The internal finish is birch-veneered plywood, with transparent acrylic windows. One problem that would need to be resolved is the lack of insulation. It could get pretty cold stuck out on a limb.

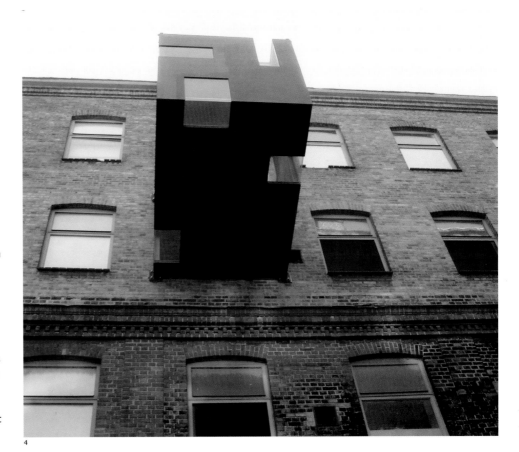

4

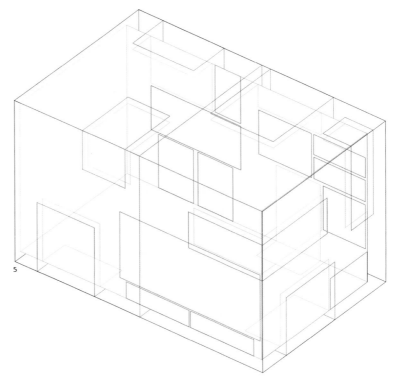

5

6 View from the Rucksack House into the host building. A large sash window acts as the entrance.

7 The Rucksack House has a floor area of 9 square metres (97 square feet). It could be used as an urban bolthole, bedroom or study.

The Rucksack House is a portable structure that is suspended from a host building which carries its weight on thick steel cables

1

1 The double bedroom is suspended from the roof and accessed from the mezzanine level of the small linear apartment. The step doubles as seating for the dining-table.

2 Section through the split-level apartment

3 In its original format the studio included only one staircase.

Suspended bedroom

Paris | France | Emmanuel Combarel Dominique Marrec Architectes | Space added: 8m² (86ft²)

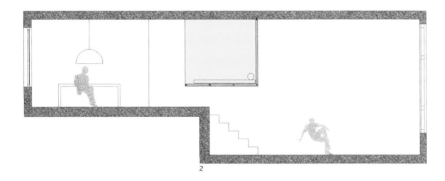

2

3

What happens when you need more space but an external extension is not an option, perhaps because your building is hemmed in by other properties, or because it is listed as a structure of historic significance? It is in such circumstances that real innovation is called for.

It was the former conundrum that faced Parisian architects Emmanuel Combarel and Dominique Marrec. In 2004, the young duo was approached by two old friends, a couple who run a fashionable contemporary art gallery, to design a bedroom inside their small apartment, a former artist's studio. There was no potential for building above, below or beside the 50-square-metre (538-square-foot) apartment. They needed to create something within the existing volume. It was a case of producing something out of nothing.

Before work began, the front door opened onto a mezzanine level enclosed by a half-height wall overlooking the main volume of the apartment, which has a roof height of 3.7 metres (12 feet). The mezzanine incorporated a small kitchen and bathroom which could not be moved without impacting prohibitively on the budget of €35,000 ($44,000). Access between the levels was via a staircase to one side of the mezzanine.

Without taking a slice out of the main living space – an option of last resort – it was very difficult to see how a bedroom could be added. Combarel and Marrec's solution was to design a steel-framed cube and suspend it from the ceiling in the centre of the apartment, with staircases either side to facilitate circulation throughout the apartment.

As well as providing an independent bedroom, the suspended cube – which has a floor area of approximately 2.8 metres by 2.8 metres (9 feet by 9 feet) – helps to dissolve the distinction between the two halves of the apartment. The step up to the bedroom also serves as additional seating at the dining-table.

'It is an object of curiosity, an anomaly,' say the architects. Conventions of privacy are reversed. The bedroom, typically a private space, is visible from the front door, meaning that the living space at the rear is secluded – views from the door are blocked.

The frame of the bedroom is clad in timber panels and finished in white polyurethane resin, to blend with the rest of the apartment.

The small addition took only three months to design and build. As well as transforming the property's viability as a living space for a couple, it has also radically enhanced its market value.

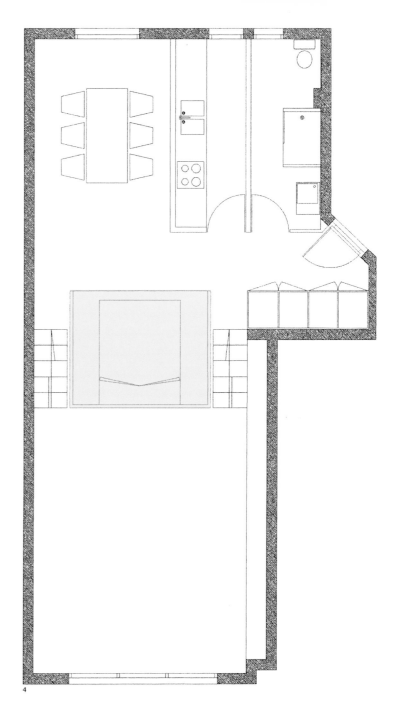

4

Practical considerations

There are few universal truths in the design of residential extensions. Budgets, timescales, functional aspirations and aesthetic preferences are as varied and eccentric as the people who commission them – not to mention the architects entrusted with their design, but there is at least one exception to the rule. Regardless of nationality or wealth, there can be few homeowners who have not at some stage wondered whether they could make their home a better place to live in by carrying out alterations or by adding an extension. The quest for space and comfort may have idiosyncratic outcomes, but the aspiration is common to millions of us.

For many, the thought-process gets no further than a daydream on the way home from work. But for others the idea becomes reality, perhaps because of a pressing need – the family is growing, or a grandparent is moving in – or a competitive urge to keep up with the neighbours.

Either way, everyone who acts on the impulse for improvement is likely to have the same questions: Do I need planning permission? How do I find an architect? What will the extension/alteration cost? Will it add value? What materials should I use? . . .

These questions and others are answered over the following pages.

Do I need planning permission?

Planning and development guidelines vary enormously between countries, cities and neighbourhoods, but as a rule of thumb, extensions that impact on a building's public façade are likely to be subject to more stringent guidelines than rear or otherwise concealed additions. However, there are many exceptions to the rule. If you are in any doubt about your rights, contact your local planning department for advice.

It is also advisable to consider how your extension will impact on your neighbours. Issues that could affect your planning application include whether the addition will overlook neighbouring gardens, and the potential for heightened rooflines to cast shadows.

Finding an architect

Many architects are appointed based on recommendations from friends or family, particularly for small-scale residential jobs. Failing that, approach your national architectural association or trade body for advice. Almost all of them have online directories of their members (see selected links below).

Typically, trade associations base initial recommendations on architects' proximity to the site, and the nature of their experience. It is then down to the client to select from those offered.

When making your decision, it is advisable to draw up a shortlist of perhaps three or four architects, and to call all of them. Ask for portfolios of their previous work, and for the contact details of former clients for additional reassurance. For many people, the choice of architect comes down to personal compatibility; it is vital that you like and trust your architect.

Once a selection has been made, agree the scope and cost of architectural services before work begins. You must also decide how involved you want your architect to be. Are you employing them to draw up initial sketches or complete drawings with structural details? Finally, before work begins, make sure that all agreements are in writing.

Links to selected architectural associations and trade bodies:

Australia
The Royal Australian Institute of Architects
www.architecture.com.au
France
Conseil National de l'Ordre des Architectes
www.architectes.org
Germany
Bund Deutscher Architekten
www.bda-architekten.de
Spain
Consejo Superior de los Colegios de Arquitectos de España CSCAE
www.cscae.com

UK
Royal Institute of British Architects
www.riba.org
USA
The American Institute of Architects
www.aia.org

Briefing an architect

An extension is only as good as the clients' ability to describe their requirements to their architect. To avoid disappointment you must explain your expectations, including the intended function and management of the space, and your preferred architectural style. For instance, do you want the extension to blend in with the existing building, or to stand out? Clarity about budgets is also vital: it will minimize the potential for cost overruns, and enable your architect to give you a realistic sense of the possibilities.

The briefing document should also specify materials, environmental sustainability features and who will be making day-to-day decisions while the extension is under construction.

For first-time clients, and even for the more experienced, it is often a good idea to develop the brief collaboratively with your architect.

What will the extension cost?

Costs are subject to a wide range of variable factors, including the accessibility of the site and the availability of labour. The following approximate figures (in US dollars) for four generic extension typologies – basement, additional level, rear extension and roof-terrace – are based on the typical costs of building in Western Europe, North America and Australasia. They are intended as a guideline only.

Basement

Expanding or retrofitting a basement is, in most circumstances, the most expensive type of extension. A 60-square-metre (650-square-foot) retrofit will typically cost in the region of $175,000–200,000. Prices come down for expanding or improving an existing basement.

Additional level

The cost of adding another level is particularly difficult to predict. Examples in this book range from $50,000 to $1.5 million.

Rear extension

Prices start at $4,000–5,000 for a self-build kit conservatory, and can rise to $150,000–175,000 for an architect-designed rear addition.

Roof-terrace

Assuming that no structural work is required to strengthen the roof, a terrace can cost as little as $10,000–20,000. However, access issues and the cost of good-quality weather-resistant materials and plants mean that costs can rise to $50,000–$120,000.

For small projects, it is often a good idea to fix the architect's fee in advance, but there are alternative approaches. Fees can also be based on daily or hourly rates, or as a percentage of the total construction cost. Regardless of which approach you adopt, be sure that you know what you are paying for, and don't forget that you can select all or part of an architect's service, from an initial design discussion through to the final delivery of the project.

For many, the cost of an extension may at first appear prohibitive. But there are a number of ways to keep prices to a minimum, including using mass-produced materials and manufacturing sections of the extension off-site to keep labour expenses down. Costs should also be considered in the context of the value that the work will add to your property, and improved liveability.

Will it add value?

The following estimates are necessarily imprecise. Note that these figures do not factor in potential long-term savings through reduced energy consumption and improved insulation.

Basement

The classic retrofit basement, which extends a house by another level, can add 20 per cent or more to a property's value. The transformation of a damp under-used cellar into a usable space can have a comparable impact.

Additional level

As is the case for basements, the addition of another level the same size as the building footprint can add 20 per cent or more to the value of a property.

Rear extension

In typical circumstances, the build cost of a rear extension – which in this context refers principally to glass-roofed lean-tos and conservatories – is only reflected in the sale value of a property for well-built and well-considered schemes. The problem is that there are so many things that can go wrong, notably poor ventilation and insulation. However, a good-quality sizeable addition of 20–25 square metres (215–270 square feet), can add between 10 and 15 per cent to the value of a house. A poor-quality job can have the opposite effect.

Roof-terrace

A roof-terrace is one of the cheaper ways of adding value. In dense urban areas the creation of outdoor space can add 10–15 per cent to the sale price.

TYPOLOGIES

The following is an introductory guide to some of the key issues to take into account when thinking about extending into the basement, building another level, adding a rear extension or commissioning a roof-terrace.

Basements

Underground extensions come in all shapes and sizes, from a fully serviced swimming pool to a toy cupboard. Almost anything is possible. However, the process can be time-consuming, messy and disruptive. It is not unknown for houses to be supported on temporary works – a process known as underpinning – to allow space for a basement to be excavated underneath.

There are two main types of subterranean extension: expanding an existing space, typically a damp, low cellar; and retrofitting a basement where none previously existed. Both involve similar hazards, including earth movement and encountering large tree-roots and boulders. Design considerations are also comparable, notably ensuring access to natural light and providing adequate drainage, ventilation and damp-proofing.

As described elsewhere, basement extensions are not cheap. However, the expense should be considered against three factors: the potential of the underpinning work to help stabilize old buildings, the value added to the property, and energy savings – it is estimated that a basement can reduce energy consumption by 10 per cent compared with houses without basements.

Another often overlooked benefit of basements it that they really do get used. Unlike lofts, stuck at the top of the building and prone to extreme temperatures, basements are climate controlled and usually only a staircase below the main living area.

But there is one word of warning. In dense urban areas, excavating or enlarging a basement will impact on your neighbours, both in the inconvenience of the construction process and in potential subsidence.

Building another level

The addition of a new level is the extension type with the greatest potential to transform the character of a building. With careful detailing and a homogenous render, an early-twentieth-century house with a pitched roof and red brick walls can be turned into a Modern-style classic with white walls and a flat roof. But before any work can begin you will need a comprehensive structural survey and planning consent. The outcomes of both will determine the dimensions of your extension and the choice of materials.

From a planning perspective, building another level is often problematic, principally because of the alteration to the front façade. One of the most common ways around this problem is to set the addition back from the front of the building, making it less visible from the ground.

Even if your home is not in a heritage area, there are likely to be strict codes to conform to. Two examples of penthouse additions featured in this book – one in Germany (pages 36–41), the other in the USA (pages 42–47) – were limited to 66 per cent and 33 per cent respectively of the total building footprint.

The second most common problem with building up is the strength of the original structure. For understandable reasons, at the time of construction not many architects think about the potential for another level to be added to a house, so in most cases the perimeter walls of a building will need to be reinforced before any work can be carried out. Your engineer will give you the details.

Typically, to accommodate another level the existing roof will be removed prior to reinforcing the walls and creating a level base. Depending on the nature of the new roof, new cross-beams may also be required.

To minimize the weight added to the building, strong lightweight materials – such as timber and hollow steel frames – are often favoured for the structural frames of new upper-storey extensions.

A new level transforms the identity of a building, not only externally but also internally. The space created allows for a complete rearrangement of the existing levels. Many people also take the opportunity to allow natural light into the interior, perhaps through a top-lit stairwell or a walk-on balcony with full-height sliding doors.

Two potential problems are over-heating and insufficient insulation. New levels are exposed to the elements, so to ensure that the space is usable all year round there must be adequate cross-ventilation for cooling during the summer, and effective insulation to retain heat during the winter.

Rear extensions

Rear extensions reflect our changed lifestyles, a fact particularly evident older houses.

The rears of houses built 100 years or more ago were often crammed with the ugly parts – kitchen, toilet, cleaning spaces, and so on – leaving the front free for entertainment and relaxation. They were also poorly connected with the outdoors.

Today things have changed. Much of family life is now conducted in the kitchen, and access to the outdoors is a sought-after commodity, which may help to explain the enduring appeal of the rear addition.

In many cases rear extensions are free of planning constraints, and this can facilitate a certain freedom of expression. For instance, if designing a fully enclosed room (or rooms) as opposed to a glazed lean-to or conservatory, many people choose to design in a distinctively different style from that of the existing

structure (see 57 South Hill Park, pages 90–95, and the Caristo House, pages 100–105).

For predominantly glazed rear additions, the question of style is less relevant. Instead, heating and ventilation become more prominent concerns. To avoid creating a freezer in the winter and a sweatbox in the summer, it is essential to use good-quality double-glazing panels (which can be expensive) and to ensure that the extension has proper ventilation – either through windows or vents. The addition should also be fully integrated with the existing house; the energy trapped in the glass extension through passive solar gain, if harnessed effectively, can be used to heat the house, thereby reducing energy bills.

Whether you opt for a glazed or an enclosed extension, you will need a concrete base, ideally flush with the ground level of the house. Minor earthworks may be required to ensure that the ground level extends into the garden.

Sliding or sliding-folding doors are popular options to ensure that the links between outside and inside are seamless. Both offer the potential to open an entire wall to the elements. But they are complex items, so it is important to employ the services of an architect or experienced contractor, especially in the preparation of the opening, which must be both structurally sound and finished to exact dimensions.

Roof-terraces

Around the world, planning departments are generally much more open-minded about roof-terraces than was the case in the 1970s and 1980s. The role that roof gardens can play in increasing biodiversity, reducing the cost of heating through improved insulation, and recycling rainwater run-off is increasingly taken into consideration. For these reasons, allied to limited ground-level space in urban areas and the relative ease of maintaining a rooftop garden, roof-terraces have never been so popular.

The first issue to consider is the strength of your roof. Can it cope with the added weight, and the permanent load of surface features? As a rule of thumb, the roofs of many parts of residential buildings in Europe and America can withstand only minimal loads, wind and perhaps a little snow, but not much more.

Before attempting any major work, it is vital to consult a structural engineer for advice.

Access is another important consideration. If your roof-terrace is going to be a fully functioning feature of the apartment, a fixed or at least pull-down staircase is a must. It is very difficult to drag large planters up ladders, which can also be a hazard for children and less mobile people.

One cash drain is the use of high-quality materials and top-class craftsmanship. Unlike traditional gardens, roof-terraces have no respite from the weather. Wind, rain and sunlight all take their toll. To avoid wind damage, ensure that all surface materials and planters are well made and securely fastened.

Project credits

50 Pilgrim's Lane, London, UK
Architect **Eldridge Smerin**
Website **www.eldridgesmerin.com**
Project Team **Nick Eldridge, Piers Smerin, Sophie Ungerer, Alison Poole**
Client **Emma and Bernard Shapero**
Main Contractor **RBS Building Services**
Quantity Surveyor **AB Associates**
Structural Engineer **Elliott Wood Partnership**
Services Engineer **E+M Tecnica**
Garden Designer **Jinny Blom**
Plywood Cladding/Spiral Staircase **AMS Joinery**
Structural Glazing/Windows **Compass Glass**
Architectural Metalwork **Bonman Engineering**
Electrical Subcontractor **Tema Electrical**
Mechanical Subcontractor **Mersch/Airconditioning**

57 South Hill Park, London, UK
Architect **Robert Dye Associates**
Website **www.robertdye.com**
Project Team **Robert Dye, Jason Coleman, Shoichi Shigeyama**
Client **private**
Client's Agent **Neale and Norden**
Main Contractor **Brenlough Building Projects**
Structural Engineer **Greig Ling Consulting Engineers**
Environmental Engineer **Camtech**
Quantity Surveyor **Denis Rooney Associates**
Planning Consultant **Ruth Blum**

Armadale House, Melbourne, Australia
Architect **Jackson Clements Burrows Pty Ltd Architects**
Website **www.jcba.com.au**
Project Team **Tim Jackson, Jon Clements, Graham Burrows, Tim Leslie, Andrew Bos**
Client **private**
Builder **A. C. Paul Constructions Pty Ltd**
Structural Consultant **Adams Consulting Engineers Pty Ltd**
Mechanical Consultant **Griepink & Ward Pty Ltd**

Artist's studio, Vidreres, Spain
Architect **Josep Llobet i Gelmá**
Email address **Sep Llobet<dakasep@coac.net>**
Project Team **Manel Fernández (structure),**

Eduard Chopo (architectural student), Núria Feijoo (architectural student), Anna Vela (architect)
Client **Jorge de los Santos**
Main Contractor **Construccions Joan Call Rovira**
Electrical and Lighting Consultant **Josep Bertran**
Carpentry **Roca Fusters**
Finishes **Jose Antonio Montero**
Metalwork **Serralleria Lluís Xicola**

Bell-Simpson House, Stirlingshire, UK
Architect **NORD Architecture**
Website **www.nordarchitecture.com**
Project Team **Robin Lee, Alastair Forbes**
Client **Mr A. Bell and Ms L. Simpson**
Main Contractor **Drummond Brown Builders Ltd**
Subcontractor **Ramage Young Ltd**

Brooklyn house, New York, USA
Architect **Baumann Architecture**
Website **www.baumannarchitecture.com**
Project Team **Philippe Baumann**
Client **Noel Wiggins, Shoshana Perry**
Main Contractor **Hamptons RMR**
Structural Engineer **Virgil Yu**
Steel Erection **New York Steel**
Landscape Contractor **Edwin Hemsley**

Caristo House, Sydney, Australia
Architect **Sam Crawford Architects**
Website **www.samcrawfordarchitects.com.au**
Project Team **Sam Crawford (principal), Jolyon Sykes (project architect)**
Client **Frank Caristo**
Builder **Frank Caristo**
Engineering Consultant **Dennis Cornell**
Landscape Architect **360 Degrees**
Interiors/Lighting/Joinery **Sam Crawford Architects**

Casa A-F, Vallvidrera, Spain
Architect **exe.arquitectura**
Website **www.exearquitectura.com**
Project Team **Jaume Valor, Elisabeth Sadurní, Marc Obradó, Laura Llimós, Marc Abril, Nelson Arango, Anna Braqué, Xabier Elduayen, Olga Dominguez**

Client **private**
Builder **Crol S.L.**

Casa pR34, Mexico City, Mexico
Architect **Rojkind Arquitectos**
Website **www.rojkindarquitectos.com**
Project Team **Michel Rojkind, Agustin Pereyra, Beatriz Díaz, Álvaro Sordo, Maria Carrillo, Gianpaolo Fusari**
Client **private**
Contractor **Factor Eficiencia, Fermín Espinosa, Ricardo Brito**
Structural Engineer **Jorge Cadena**

CG Annexe, Caldetas, Spain
Designer **Francesc Rifé**
Website **www.rife-design.com**
Architect **Clara Guilera Sarda-Fortuny**
Client **CG**
Main Contractor **Buch Asociado S.L.**
Carpentry **Fusteria y Ebanisteria Brañas S.L.**
Lighting **Cronek**
Metalwork **Talleres Colmenero S.L.**
Flooring – Wood **Park House Studio**

Clifton Hill rear extension, Melbourne, Australia
Architect **Adam Dettrick**
Website **www.adamdettrickarchitect.com.au**
Project Team **Adam Dettrick**
Client **A. Hogan and I. Wilcox**
Main Contractor **Malbac Pty Ltd**
Building Surveyor **McKenzie Group Consulting**
Engineer **Robin Blien & Associates**
Landscaping **Celtic Horticultural Services**

Dirk Cove House, County Cork, Ireland
Architect **Níall McLaughlin**
Website **www.niallmclaughlin.com**
Project Team **Níall McLaughlin, Spencer Guy, Gus Lewis**
Client **private**
Client's Agent **Stephen Jeffrey of the County Homesearch Company**
Structural Engineer **Toby McLean of Packman Lucas Structural Designers**
Landscape Consultant **Peter Fitzgerald**

Dragspelhuset (Accordian House), Lake Övre Gla, Sweden
Architect 24H Architecture
Website www.24h.eu
Project Team Maartje Lammers, Boris Zeisser (principals-in-charge), Olav Bruin, Jeroen ter Haar, Sabrina Kers, Fieke Poelman
Client Zeisser family
Structural Engineer ABT (Walter Spangenberg and Wiljan Houweling)

Dr Gabka House, Munich, Germany
Architect Landau + Kindelbacher Architekten
Website www.landaukindelbacher.com
Project Team Gerhard Landau, Ludwig Kindelbacher, Lene Jünger
Client Prof. Dr. med. habil Christian Gabka
Main Contractor Hau Bauunternehmen GmbH
Structural Engineers Guggenbichler + Waganstaller
Landscape Architect Zuckschwert + Martin
Carpentry Daxenberger GmbH
Masonry Gerhard Schmitz GmbH

Duane Street Live/Work Space, New York, USA
Architect Marpillero Pollak Architects
Website www.newyork-architects.com/mparchitects
Project Team Sandro Marpillero AIA (partner-in-charge), Linda Pollak AIA and Paul Teng (project management), Alison Crawshaw, Jessica Levin, Alex Jiaravanont, Kyungen Kim
Client Marpillero and Pollak
Builders Angel Vazquez, Eric Asudillo, Alberto Paez
Structural System Damo Construction (steel structure), Metalforms (steel windows and doors to garden), Security Iron (garden steel deck and railings)
Glazing Parthenon Glass

Frankfort House, Brussels, Belgium
Architect Atelier d'Architecture Pierre Hebbelinck S.A. / Pierre Hebbelinck – Pierre de Wit – Architectes
Website www.pierrehebbelinck.net
Project Team Pierre Hebbelinck, Jean-Michel Sojic, Margarida Serrão, Gilles Honoré
Client Aline Frankfort
Main Contractor Dereymaeker B sprl
Stability Beg
Carpentry/Frame TPB S.A.
Roof Covering D'Heur et Fils

Furniture Maker's Bedroom, Lille, France
Architect Isabelle Menu and Luc Saison
Email address lsaison@club-internet.fr
Project Team Mancy Lor, Nicolas Villemin
Client Mr and Mrs Leblan
Contractor Loison Company

House Ray 1, Vienna, Austria
Architect Delugan Meissl Associated Architects
Website www.deluganmeissl.at
Project Team Anke Goll, Christine Hax, Martin Josst
Client Delugan Meissl
Main Contractor Baumeister Tupy GmbH
Structural Consultant Werkraum Wien
Façade Kusolitsch Aluminium- u. Stahlkonstruktionen
Steel Construction Buttazoni GmbH
Sheet Membrane Roofing DWH Dach & Wand Huemer + Co GmbH
Waterproofing Willich Trochenbau GmbH
Service Lines/Electrical Planning Friedrich Hess GmbH
Carpentry Franz Walder GmbH
Lighting Erco, Guzzini
Mountings Dornbracht
Kitchen Equipment Smeg
Ventilation Trox
Furniture Delugan Meissl Associated Architects, Vitra (Charles and Ray Eames), Fritz Hansen (Arne Jacobsen), Moroso (Patricia Urquiola)

Lee Residence, La Jolla, California, USA
Architect Public
Website www.publicdigital.com
Project Team James Gates and James Brown (principals), Steve Rosenstein, Francisco Garcia
Client Kim and Torrey Lee
Main Contractor Public
Project Team Michael P. Paluso, Alfred Wilson, Jeff Burns, Ojay Pagano, Jonathon Stevens, Chris Robitaille, Eric Nation, Matt Maze, Alex Young
Structural Consultant Envision Engineering
Mechanical, Electrical and Plumbing Consultant Salehi and Salehi

Lightweight penthouse, Stuttgart, Germany
Architect Hartwig N. Schneider Architekten
Website www.hartwigschneider.de
Project Team Dennis Mueller, Ingo Pelchen, Almut Schwabe
Client private
Concrete Contractor Wolff & Müller

Steel Construction Mayer Metalbau
Plasterer Anton Geiselhart (exterior plus light walls)

Loftcube, Germany
Architect Werner Aisslinger
Website www.aisslinger.de
Project Team Studio Aisslinger
Client Studio Aisslinger
Main Sponsor DuPont
Collaborators Zanotta, Interlübke, DuPont (finishes Corian, Zodiaq, Antron)

Manhattan roof-terrace, New York, USA
Architect Studio Rinaldi
Website www.studiosrinaldi.com
Project Team Stefania Rinaldi (principal), Brian Liona, Aurelio Clementi, Dara Burke, Daniel Hammerman, Beatrice Popoiu, Tavis Wright
Client private
General Contractor William Dorvillier
Engineering Consultant Elie Geiger
Landscape Architect Story (Paula Hayes, principal)

New Cabaña, Girona, Spain
Architect Hidalgo Hartmann
Project Team Jordi Hidalgo Tané (architect), Daniela Hartmann (interior architect)
Client Lluis and Montserrat
Main Contractor/Construction Company Construccions Santa Pau S.L.

Patio House, Nantes, France
Architect Michelle Pasquier
Email address michellepasquier@wanadoo.fr
Project Team Michelle Pasquier, Marco Tabet (architectural assistant)
Client M. and Mme Donias
Main Contractor De Carvalho

Photographer's penthouse, New York, USA
Architect Christoff:Finio Architecture
Website www.christofffinio.com
Project Team Martin Finio and Taryn Christoff (principals-in-charge); Robert Donnelly, Tanja Sussman, Alexander Huerzeler, Noah Biklen
Client Jan Staller
Main Contractor Skylight Interior Construction
Structural Contractor Buro Happold
Mechanical Contractor Mec-Con Associates

Rear family room, London, UK
Architect Map Projects Ltd

Website www.mapprojects.com
Project Team Pasquale Amodio with Diego
Bortolato, Randa Hanna, Jonathan Rowley
Client Jasmeen Zafar and Matthew Hutchings
Main Contractor Ian and Duncan Campbell @
Vision Contractors
Structural Engineers Packman Lucas Structural
Designers
Party Wall Surveyors Delva Patman Associates

Rooftop bedrooms, Montrouge, France
Architect Tectône
Website www.tectone.net
Project Team Pascal Chombart de Lauwe and
Sabri Bendimérad (architects), Jean Thibault
Bernard (architectural assistant)
Client private
Main Contractor Concept & Réalisation
Wooden Structure Barcque

Rucksack House – Courtesy Fiedler
Contemporary, Cologne, Germany
Architect Stefan Eberstadt
Website c/o www.ulrichfiedler.com
Project Team Stefan Eberstadt (artist), Courtney
Smith
Client Stefan Eberstadt in collaboration with Dr.
Klaus Röckerath, represented by Mahlburg Real
Estate, Cologne
Main Contractor Alfred Mayrhofer (Dobetsberger)
Structural Engineer Thomas Bec, a.k.a Ingenieure
Collaborating Engineers Hans-Günter Schäfer
(IS Engineers Office, Netzwerk im Bauturm),
Barbara Katrin Schaeffer, Octavianne Hornstein,
Alfred Karner
Funders Fiedler Contemporary, Cologne (www.
ulrichfiedler.com), Stiftung Federkiel/Halle 14,
Leipzig (www.federkiel.org), Project Fellowship
for the Arts in 2004 by the City of Munich Plan
Project, Cologne (www.plan-project.com)

Santa Barbara Ranch House, Santa Barbara,
California, USA
Architect Nick Noyes Architecture
Website www.nnarchitecture.com
Project Team Nick Noyes, Scott Baltimore
Client Richard and Lloyd Dallet
Contractor William A. Below General Contractor

Solar Umbrella, Venice, California, USA
Architect Pugh + Scarpa
Website www.pugh-scarpa.com

Project Team Lawrence Scarpa and Angela
Brooks (principals-in-charge), Anne Burke,
Vanessa Hardy, Ching Luk, Gwynne Pugh
Client Lawrence Scarpa and Angela Brooks
General Contractor Above Board Construction
Structural Engineer Gwynne Pugh of Pugh + Scarpa

Symbiont Friedrich extension, Merzig,
Germany
Architect FloSundK architektur + urbanistik
Website www.flosundk.de
Project Team Achour Belhouchat, Martin Prölsz
Client Patrick and Sabah Friedrich
Statics IBL Baustatik

Suspended bedroom, Paris, France
Architect Emmanuel Combarel Dominique
Marrec Architectes
Website www.combarel-marrec.com
Project Team Antoine Pradels (assistant architect)
Client private

Tall Acres, Pittsford, New York, USA
Architect Studio for Architecture
Website www.studioforarchitecture.net
Project Team Mehrdad Hadighi (project
architect), Israel Lowry (project assistant)
Client Dr Mohammad Salahuddin and Dr Anwara
Begum
Construction Contractor Russ Sinacori (Cori
Construction)

Terrace and swimming pool, Nantes, France
Architect Mûrisserie Parent-Rachdi
Website murisserie.ath.cx/
Project Team Sonia Rachdi, Yves Parent, Claire
Lallié, Aymeric Trutet
Client private
General Contractor Loreau
Wood Construction Demangeau
Metal Construction Cobaplis
Cladding Raimond
Waterproofing Face Atlantique
Woodwork and Plastering SER
Tiling Girard (house), André (swimming pool)
Electricity Legrand
Plumbing and Ventilation Legrand
Wall-to-wall Carpet Tarquett Sommer
Soft Flooring Forbo Sarlino
Exterior Paving Granil-Flandre
Interior Wall and Ceiling Tiling CINCVA
Paintwork Caparol

Underground entertainment space, London,
UK
Architect Granit Chartered Architects
Website www.granit.co.uk
Project Team Robert Wilson (architectural
director), James Munro (architect), Alex
Dusterloh (architectural assistant)
Client private
Main Contractor RCL
Engineers Price & Meyers
Interior Designer Georgie Maw
Glass Doors Solarlux
Glass Works Glazeguard
Stonework Stone Productions

Vermont Avenue House, Moss Beach,
California, USA
Architect Aidlin Darling Design
Website www.aidlindarlingdesign.com
Project Team Joshua Aidlin, David Darling
Client Tena and Erik Watts
General Contractor McVay Construction
Structural Engineer SDE

Villa 57+, Dortmund, Germany
Architect ArchiFactory.de
Website www.archifactory.de
Project Team Matthias Herrmann, Matthias Koch
Client Michael Köppen
Construction Management ArchiFactory.de
Structural Engineer Assmann Beraten und Planen

Villa at Lake Bled, Slovenia
Architect Ofis Arhitekti
Website www.ofis-a.si
Project Team Rok Oman, Špela Videčnik, Mladen
Bubalo, Rok Gerbec, Ivana Sehic, Karla Murovec
Client private

Violin House, Melbourne, Australia
Architect Cassandra Complex
Website www.cassandracomplex.com.au
Project Team Cassandra Fahey (architect),
Matthew Bird, Scott Woodward
Client Josh Abrahams
Main Contractor R & G Smith Pty Ltd
Custom Fireplace Surrounding Tiles and Hand Basins
Josh Rowell (potter/artist)
Tetris Green Tiles Arte Domus (design by
Cassandra Complex), manufactured by Domus
Ceramics (Aust) Pty Ltd

Index

Page numbers in *italics* refer to picture captions.

Picture credits

The publishers would like to thank the following sources for permission to reproduce images in this book.

Courtesy 24H Architecture (225)
Courtesy ArchiFactory.de (188-191)
Courtesy Atelier d'Architecture Pierre Hebbelinck* S.A. (171 right)
Claus Bach (237, 240-241)
Sue Barr/VIEW (90, 92-95)
Courtesy Baumann Architecture (27)
Gaston Bergeret (242, 245)
Brett Boardman (100, 102-105)
Richard Bryant/ARCAID (10)
Eduardo Calderon (16)
Courtesy Cassandra Complex (79)
Courtesy Christoff:Finio Architecture (43 left)
Courtesy Emmanuel Combarel Dominique Marrec Architectes (243)
Courtesy Sam Crawford (101)
Courtesy Aidlin Darling Design (67 left)
Julien de Bock@map architects (122-125)
Courtesy Adam Dettrick (107 left)
Lyndon Douglas (140, 141 right, 142-145)
J.P. Duplan/Lightmotiv (32-34)
Courtesy Robert Dye Associates (91)
Stefan Eberstadt (238)
Edifice/Emily Cole (8 right)
Edifice/Gillian Dorley (8 left)
Edifice/Philippa Lewis (9)
Courtesy Eldridge Smerin (141 left)
Courtesy Foster and Partners (12)
Dennis Gilbert/VIEW (6)
Jeff Goldberg/ESTO (200, 202, 205)
John Gollings (17, 20- 4; 78, 81-83)
Courtesy Granit Chartered Architects (61 left)
Tomaz Gregoric (72-77)
Mehrdad Hadighi (132-136)
Courtesy Hardwig n. Schneider freie architekten bda (36-41)
Michael Heinrich (196-201)
Courtesy David Hewitt and Anne Garrison (110, 114-115)
Courtesy Hildalgo Hartmann (176 top)
Hertha Hurnaus (48, 50 top left, 54)
Steffen Jaenicke (230-235)
Nicholas Kane (164-169)
D.I. Angelo Kaunat (11 left)
G.G. Kirchner (84-87)
Silke Koch (241)
Andrew Lee (96-99)
Courtesy Josep Llobet (146)
Courtesy Marpillero Pollak Architects (201)

J.M. Monthiers (56, 59)
Courtesy Mûrisserie Parent-Rachdi (211 top)
Courtesy The Museum of the City of New York (11 middle)
Jaime Navarro (218-223)
Courtesy Nick Noyes Architecture (183)
Killian O'Sullivan of Light Room Architectural Photography (60, 61 right, 62-65)
Alfonso Paredes (26, 29-31)
Courtesy Michelle Pasquier (116-118)
J.D. Peterson Photography (182, 185-187)
Marie-Françoise Plissart (170, 171 left, 172-175)
Eugeni Pons (147-151, 152-156, 158-163, 176 bottom-181)
Courtesy Public (15, 111-113)
Courtesy Pugh + Scarpa (127)
Marvin Rand (126, 128-131)
Christian Richters (224, 226-231)
Peter Rigaud (49)
Philippe Ruault (119, 210, 211 bottom, 213-215)
Michal Ronnen Safdie (11 right)
Bill Sanders (14)
Margherita Spilluttini (13 top)
Jan Staller (42, 43 right - 46)
Rupert Steiner (2, 50 top right, 50 bottom, 52-53, 55)
Tim Street-Porter/ESTO (13 bottom)
John Sutton (66, 67 right, 68-71)
Derek Swallwell (106, 107 right-109)
Thomas Taubert (236)
Courtesy Tectône (57)
Wade Zimmerman (207-209)